Heroes
Among Us

Heroes Among Us

Social Entrepreneurs
Strengthening Families and
Building Communities

Peter Heegaard

edited by Lori Sturdevant

NODIN PRESS

ISBN 978-1-932472-67-7

Library of Congress control number: 2008932991

The author wishes to acknowledge the support of the
Urban Adventure Fund at the Minneapolis Foundation.
Royalties received by the author that exceed expenses will
be donated to the non-profit organizations featured in
this book.

Design: John Toren

Nodin Press, LLC
530 North Third Street
Suite 120
Minneapolis, MN
55401

This book is dedicated to my wife Anne, who has been my incredibly wonderful partner for more than fifty years, and to the remarkable individuals whose stories follow.

Contents

ACKNOWLEDGEMENTS

First and foremost, I want to thank the storytellers included in this book for taking the time from very busy schedules to share their stories. In nearly every case I have known and admired these individuals for many years. Several were new acquaintances who were referred to me by other leaders in the Twin Cities. The process involved visiting with each of them for at least three to four hours, taping their life histories, transcribing the tapes for their review, and editing for clarity and continuity. It has taken five years to complete this work.

I owe a great debt to my editor Lori Sturdevant, who gave up weekends to review these stories and offered much-needed advice on how to structure this project so that the intellectual and emotional intent of the storytellers was clear to the reader. This process is new to me and the editorial enhancements are significant indeed. Then of course my thanks to publisher Norton Stillman and his associate John Toren. Norton loves this community and was willing to take a risk on an untested author. He also happens to share with me the early life experience of growing up in south Minneapolis and attending John Burroughs School.

There are a number of individuals I would like to acknowledge and thank for helping me become acquainted with these social entrepreneurs. Because the community leaders whose stories follow have been willing to share so much about the people and events that helped influence their thinking, I thought it would be appropriate to reflect on a few of the individuals who have helped shape my own values.

My first exposure to political and social issues came at the Blake School from a well known history teacher and debate coach named Jack Edie. Jack was a true educator in that he required the analysis of both the pros and cons of a social issue with the final admonition that we must reach a conclusion and offer a specific recommendation. Later at Dartmouth College this discipline was reinforced by a senior year course named "Great Issues," which, in addition to bringing world leaders from all political perspectives to campus, required that we pick a topic and follow its reporting by six newspapers offering different points of view.

There were two professors in graduate school at The Amos Tuck School of Business Administration who had a profound impact on my understanding of what it takes to be successful at community building. The first was Wayne Broehl Jr. who taught a course on business ethics. I believe this was one of the first (1958) of its kind in the United States. The intent was to illustrate that business relies upon many constituencies and that an investment by companies in a healthy community infrastructure was not inconsistent with building shareholder value for its owners. The other was John Hennesey, who taught a course dealing with sound management administrative practices. John taught us that when dealing with person-to-person communication issues, it was important to view the issue, and also yourself, through the eyes of the other person before reaching your own conclusion and committing to a course of action. In effect it was a course on empathy and objectivity, and over the years I have found these to be invaluable tools in dealing with a wide range of community-building efforts.

When Anne and I moved back to Minneapolis in 1960 after graduate school and a stint in the army, we shopped around for a church. We found an activist church in Deephaven, Minnesota, St. Luke Presbyterian Church, that believed in studying social issues, sharing through dialogue what we had learned, and finally committing to some form of both group and personal social action. The minister, Robert Hudnut, was not at all bashful about challenging each of us to become involved with both direct service non-profit organizations and federations and political entities that promoted social change. This experience exposed us both to a host of effective social service and social action organizations. The turbulent 1960s had a profound influence on us both.

This same activist spirit continued at our church under the leadership of Richard Lundy, who took the process a step further by leading St. Luke Church to declare itself a "Sanctuary Church." This was in the early 1980s during the period when individuals from Central America who opposed their oppressive governments were forced to flee for their lives. One such individual, Rene Hertado, came to St. Luke under threat of death from extremists on both the political left and right in El Salvador. Many such refugees who were forcibly returned home never lived to see their families again. The risks to which a congregation exposed itself by sheltering such an individual were high indeed. Now, twenty-five years later, Rene Hertado has finally achieved legal status in the United States. This experience opened our eyes to the many challenges faced by these refugees. The stories of two such individuals who went on to significantly enriched our community are included in this book.

Early in my career at what was then known as the Northwestern National Bank of Minneapolis, I received a phone call from a Mr. Philip Brain who was employed by the YMCA. He was also a key volunteer for the Community Chest (later to be renamed as the Greater Twin Cities United Way). Phil asked if I would head up an effort to call on all of the bars and restaurants in downtown Minneapolis. I never asked Phil why he thought I was especially well-qualified for this particular task. Nevertheless this effort exposed me to more than one hundred charitable organizations that serve disadvantaged individuals and families in the region. Phil, one of the last survivors of the Bataan Death March, and his wife Deloris, became partners with us in a cabin in northern Minnesota. His stories of how he managed psychologically and physically to survive under brutal conditions in death camps instilled in all who knew him a deep sense of appreciation for life and the things that make community work.

One of my long time friends, Jim Martineau, exposed me to an organization called The Citizen's League shortly after we moved back to the Twin Cities in 1960. Headed up in those days by Ted Kolderie and Paul Gilje, former reporters for the

Minneapolis Star Tribune, the league had a discipline where you joined a group that studied a local civic issue, sorted out key "findings," moved on to reaching "conclusions," and finally submitted "recommendations" to elected officials, the media, and the organization's membership. I am especially grateful to those founders, including Anne's father, Bradshaw Mintener, and supporters of the league who helped so many of us develop a more professional approach to civic engagement.

One of my prime mentors at the Northwestern National Bank of Minneapolis was Leonard Ramberg, who oversaw economic development and civic engagement. Leonard was a highly respected community leader, and helped set the stage for corporate values that required that employees be involved in some aspect of community building. This was at a time when suburban growth was rapid and a host of new urban issues were coming to the forefront.

My four older brothers, Bill, Roger, John, and David, have each in their own way served as role models for me. We grew up with parents who were politically quite conservative, but when faced directly with someone in need of immediate help they were quick to respond with assistance. I am sure those values rubbed off on each of us. Our children, Susan, Kip, and Kate, were very tolerant of Anne and me during their early teen years when we dragged them off to meetings of the Handicapped Federation, Senior Citizen's Federation, and a host of other civically engaged organizations that served disadvantaged populations. We have a large immediate and extended family and I am so very grateful for the support they have all given to Anne and me.

Finally once again I must thank Anne for supporting me in pulling together these stories. It was during our early married years that she got me involved in an urban issues training program called "The Women's Institute for Social Change." This was a program sponsored by The Junior League of Minneapolis, an exclusively women's organization. One of their goals was to encourage leaders in business and the professions to get away from their offices for a few hours each month and take a look at what is going on with the lives of less fortunate folks in the community. Anne has been instrumental in helping me structure "Urban Adventure," the urban issues program I have managed for financial executives since I retired from the investment business (Lowry Hill, a subsidiary of Wells Fargo) in 1996. The social entrepreneurs whose stories follow could not have been identified without the support of all of the individuals I have mentioned plus many others which I lack the space and time to include. My heartfelt thanks to all of these individuals who have helped open my eyes to the magic of community building and the incredible men and women who make it happen.

Peter Heegaard

INTRODUCTION

What type of individual would enter a field of work where the risks were high and the economic rewards low? Why, for example, would an attorney start a law firm, attract other bright lawyers to work with him, experience enormous success, and then begin to devote so many hours to pro-bono work that his partners asked him to leave? Douglas Hall made just such a mid-life shift, and went on to found the Legal Rights Center, which has proven to be the leading defender in the Upper Midwest of poor and disadvantaged members of the community—including those charged with felonies. I served on and chaired the board of this center for several years, and that brought me into contact with leaders in the African American, Native American, Asian and Hispanic communities. It was the gift of this experience, and the example of Doug Hall and others, that opened my eyes to the remarkable work of the many social entrepreneurs who have had a profound influence on the Twin Cities community.

My own working career began in 1960 at what was then known as the Northwestern National Bank of Minneapolis in the field of investments, betting risk capital on both emerging and established companies. I found that more often than not, the largest rewards came from startup companies that had the potential to someday dominate their industries, created by entrepreneurs who were willing to risk their own capital to launch a new venture. The risks were high, but so were the rewards. The stories that follow offer clues as to why certain individuals with equally strong leadership qualities follow a different path, choosing to face similar risks and demands in pursuit of goals that offer far less scope for personal financial reward. The individuals portrayed in the following pages have developed not-for-profit organizations. They have become successful social entrepreneurs.

The expression "social entrepreneur" is not a new one—it began to appear in the literature of social change during the early 1970s—but it may be unfamiliar to some readers. In recent times it has been applied to a range of activities stretching from Nobel laureate Muhammad Yumas's "capitalist revolution" of micro-credit, to Steve Jobs's highly profitable ways of transforming individual lives through electronic innovations. It might be helpful for us to consider that unlike other social service workers, a social entrepreneur recognizes and seizes upon new ways to solve long-standing problems, often exploring new methods and ideals at considerable personal risk. Yet unlike a traditional entrepreneur, the social entrepreneur pursues goals that lie in the social sphere, far beyond simple calculations of monetary return on investment. The methods are creative and business-like, the ends are social and ameliatory.

My wife Anne and I have long been involved in supporting Minnesota's non-profit organizations. Our interest was nurtured by a liberal arts education, involvement in a socially active church, some incredible mentors, and a general sense that we would like to share the good luck we've experienced with others. Along the way we've become friends with some remarkable leaders in the not-for-profit community. They have inspired us, and because of their great talent and skill, made me grateful that I did not have to compete with them in the for-profit world.

One experience shortly after we returned to Minneapolis from the Army in 1960 had a lasting impact on us. One Sunday our minister, Robert Hudnut, challenged the congregation to either be part of a group visiting the local nursing home, or to spend one night a week for four weeks at the women's correctional facility for Hennepin County known as the Work House. Anne and I opted for the latter, and wound up playing the card game Whist with women doing time for prostitution. During out conversations we learned that to move these women into mainstream society would require educating them, finding them work, and moving them to a community where the local pimp could not control them. In other words, it would take leadership, money, and a systemic approach to getting the job done right. This simple lesson, and others like it, re-focused our attention on what other men and women were already doing locally to plan, organize, and lead not-for-profit organizations that attacked tough social problems, and it has stayed with us throughout the nearly fifty years we have been active in the community. Working with these amazing leaders became our prime avocation, and it has enriched our lives immeasurably.

What follows are stories about men and women who have started or successfully built non-profit organizations to the point where they have become leaders in their respective fields. The stories herein are not about those organizations per se, but about the characters, motivations, sensitivities, values, and ambitions of the women and men who have led them. In each case, the organizations they have managed have improved the lives of thousands of people. They cover a wide range of not-for-profit activity. The people you will meet on the pages that follow have provided legal representation and advocacy for low-income people charged with crimes. They've built professionalism in the criminal justice system, at all levels. They've constructed affordable housing that includes the essential social and economic support systems to keep chronically homeless people well housed. They've trained and found work for new immigrants in the Asian and African American communities. They've identified and prepared low-income residents of all ethnic backgrounds to become for-profit entrepreneurs, leading the economic revival of deteriorating commercial corridors. They've trained and established broadcasting capability within Native American communities. They've taught job skills and created employment for physically and mentally handicapped men and women, advanced the careers of women at the executive level in government, furthered entrepreneurialism within the Hispanic community, and empowered women who have been abused and dehumanized to become self-sufficient, productive citizens.

These stories in many ways resemble mysteries. They provide hints and clues about the circumstances, environmental conditions, and sheer serendipity that give birth to and nurture success in social entrepreneurship. Each individual portrayed here appears to have been born with an entrepreneurial gift. Yet I believe readers will find a pattern in these stories of luck and skill entwined in a symbiotic way. The proportions vary from story to story, but none of these entrepreneurs succeeded with either talent or serendipity alone.

A second element appears in story after story: early in their experiences, these individuals almost without exception benefited from mentors who helped them identify and develop their gifts in such a way as to become effective community leaders. Many of them came from middle-class families that had been sensitized by the hardships of the mid-twentieth century, and had benefited from a neighborhood support system. Each appears to have a solid sense of self and an eagerness to relish new experiences. While widely different in style, they each have a strong work ethic and ability to persist, despite adversity in their personal lives. There is also a sense of playfulness in the way many of them approach life—an ability to see the humor in their own shortcomings and those of others as they struggle with an unceasing barrage of challenges. Despite the serious nature of their work, they make the game fun, which is essential in motivating a staff that in nearly every case could earn more money working in the for-profit world. To a person, these individuals possess strong leadership and managerial skills. In nearly every case, they built organizations that have thrived and continued to grow, even after their own retirement.

Our world clearly needs to develop more leaders who can follow in the footsteps of the individuals described in the pages of this book, women and men with the combination of compassion, management skills, entrepreneurial drive and creativity required to keep our society healthy. I have been personally inspired by leaders such as Jim Shannon, who was president of the College of Saint

Thomas, and went on to head both the Minneapolis and General Mills Foundations; Russ Ewald, who led the McKnight Foundation into imaginative and challenging new areas of community building; Elmer L. Andersen, who moved Minnesota forward as governor, chair of the University of Minnesota Board of Regents and in so many other ways; W. Harry Davis, the unchallenged leader of the African American community, who taught us persistence and tolerance; and Joe Selvaggio who started the City Inc., Project for Pride in Living, the One Percent Club and more recently Micro Grants, all organizations working to improve our community. The books written about their lives and social commitment sparked my interest in recording the autobiographies of social entrepreneurs whose stories have not yet been told.

A number of signs suggest that in recent years, Minnesotans may have become more disassociated from one another. Our economic specialization, self-reliant philosophy, and self-indulgent lifestyles distract us from attending to the basic building blocks that have traditionally maintained healthy societies. If you have read *The Emigrants* or *Giants in the Earth*, you will recall the challenges experienced by Scandinavian and German settlers in the Upper Midwest. They endured severe hardship as they traveled by ox cart, ship, rail and foot to settle in Minnesota. They found they needed to form societies and cooperatives to support one another and organize for the common good. There appeared to be a healthy balance in their lives between self-reliance and community building. Life was tough indeed, but they were able to pass on a rich heritage to those of us who followed. It's up to us to maintain a positive balance between personal gain and the common good in our own time. I believe the people whose stories are told here have found that balance, and can show the way for future generations.

History is full of examples of societies that failed through lack of attention to the common good. The lack of shared values and a healthy common vision for the future were often at the root of economic and social collapse. In addition, leaders failed to emerge who could mediate between a mature society's many competing factions. My hope is that these stories will convey a better understanding of leadership and the critical role it plays in the nonprofit sector of Minnesota's social and economic system. I find their stories fascinating and uplifting and I believe you will too. If you are inspired to action by the example of these social entrepreneurs, so much the better.

In the text that follows, you'll find my own words in bold type and the first-person account of each of my subjects in regular type. My desire was to avoid the complication of repeated quotation marks. You'll also find at the book's end a glossary of Minnesota leaders whose names appear with some frequency in these accounts. Identifying information about those important Minnesotans is provided there, rather than as a frequent interruption of the stories being told.

DOUGLAS HALL

You go to these meetings and someone says, "I don't really understand how democracy is supposed to work," and you can show them that it really is built from the ground up, bit by bit. It really grabs hold of you. I have been amazed.

– Douglas Hall, June 2003

The violent, turbulent late 1960s demanded new and creative leadership. The Twin Cities were fortunate indeed that the right leaders emerged at just the right time. 1968 was the year that both Robert Kennedy and Martin Luther King were assassinated and the Vietnam war was sparking student demonstrations across the country. On the near north side of Minneapolis, it was a year of an uneasy, wary truce, following a riot in the summer of 1967 that had left many of the area's businesses in flames.

The Legal Rights Center was founded by Douglas Hall, Syl Davis, and Clyde Bellecourt in 1970 as the first non-profit community-based law firm in the Upper Midwest devoted to serving disadvantaged populations, including those charged with felonies. Doug Hall was white and well educated. He had founded (and had later walked out of) a well-established Minneapolis law firm. Syl Davis was black and a recognized leader of the emerging activist African American community. Clyde Bellecourt was one

1

of a handful of young, aggressive Native American leaders who started the American Indian Movement (AIM)—some of whose leaders gained notoriety for participating in the shoot-out with federal officers at Wounded Knee, South Dakota, in February 1973.

The Legal Rights Center was formed to defend low-income people of color and help them deal with conditions that put them at risk of arrest, such as unemployment, chemical dependency, learning disabilities, and mental illness. The Center is unique in the role it gives to community workers in the African American, Native American, Hispanic, and Asian communities. They make the initial contact with a potential client, review the case, and assign it to one of the center's lawyers as warranted. Federal Judge Michael Davis and Hennepin County District Judge Pamela Davis are former center attorneys, which speaks well for the center's reputation in the legal community.

Doug Hall was in his late eighties when I sat with him and his wife Mary in their farmhouse near Wabasha in southeastern Minnesota on June 6, 2003. It was a beautiful spring day. The view extended off across the newly planted fields and the entire expanse of Lake Pepin toward the far-off limestone bluffs on the Wisconsin side.

Hall's medical prognosis called for several more years of quality life, but that proved to be too optimistic. He was diagnosed with pancreatic cancer in the fall of 2004 and died shortly thereafter. Doug used a walker that day, and I recorded as he sat in a comfortable lounge chair with his golden retriever by his side. Mary, Doug's wife and partner in his life's work, sat across from him as he spoke. She interjected tidbits of fascinating background about community life at the time. I've included many of Mary's comments about the political and social climate that shaped Doug's values and clearly influenced his work. Their relationship was very close. Mary provided the intellectual, emotional, and financial support that allowed Doug to devote his later years to pro-bono legal work.

Doug became emotional when he recalled episodes of racism and anti-Semitism in his early life. Tears rolled down his cheeks as he described the abuse at college that destroyed a beautiful and talented Jewish girl he had known in high school. He was saddened by what he perceived as a relapse in this country's commitment to human rights in this decade. Yet his belief in the inherent goodness of people kept him hopeful about the future. What Doug Hall and the Legal Rights Center accomplished in convincing a large segment of both the Native American and African American communities that they would at least get a hearing if they participated in the criminal justice system is nothing short of amazing.

Doug: I was born in 1915, and Mary was born in 1916. My mother, Violet, was a very gentle, kind, loving person. I don't think I ever heard her express a political view in her life. She was a Christian Scientist. Her mother, Grandmother Hart, was a Christian Science practitioner. Mother was a second reader in the major Christian Science church in Grand Rapids. I had a brother, Robert, who died shortly after birth, and an older sister. I got into a real jangle when I decided I wanted a middle name. They hadn't given me one. So I took Robert as my middle name. That was at the time that I wanted a bike. So we ordered a bike from Sears Roebuck in Chicago. I wrote Douglas Robert Hall on the ownership claim. Eventually Mother got a call asking, "Is there a Douglas Robert Hall there?" She replied, "No, we don't have anybody by that name," and I almost lost my bike!

My dad, Clare, was a lawyer in private practice, and in later years he became a specialist in natural gas development in Michigan. He became attorney for the Grand Rapids gas company, and then for its holding company in Detroit. He was very conservative. As I recall, he was the "bag man" for the Republican Party and delivered money around for various campaigns. He gave me a good background in American history.

My dad was a bigot, plain and simple, be it blacks, Indians,

Catholics, or Jews. However, he shared a law office with Gus Wolf, a brilliant Jewish attorney, for twenty-five or thirty years. They never had a partnership, but they shared office space and were very close friends. In the years immediately after my mother died, Dad traveled around the globe with Gus. I finally said to him, after I got up enough nerve, "How can you call Jewish people Kikes, and still have Gus as your best friend?" "Never could happen again!" he shouted.

Dad and I were great baseball fans. We went several times a year to Detroit to watch major league ball. When Jackie Robinson came to the major leagues in 1947, my dad said to me the exact same thing that one of the star Brooklyn players put to Dodgers general manager Branch Rickey: "Mr. Rickey, do you really think they are human?"

The first realization I had of the injustice of this whole racial and ethnic picture was in high school. One of the outstanding persons among my high school classmates, academically and personality-wise, was Elise Mayer, whose father was Jewish and mother Protestant. She was just kind of a queen. She graduated the same time I did, and went to college at Ann Arbor. At that time the women in the freshman year were all put in dormitories. She was put in a dormitory called "Mosher-Jordan." The campus name for it was "Kosher-Jordan." That broke her heart, and she dropped out. That was one of the first real jolts I got during my first year in college. It hurt.

The other individual that was central to my awakening was Bernard Jefferson. The school district included part of the ghetto, so we had black students in our high school class. Jefferson was a phenomenal athlete in football, basketball, and track. He was an above-average student, and was involved in extracurricular things like YMCA. He was a very popular student, but he was also the butt of a lot of bad humor. He had long arms and hands, and kids would compare him to a guerilla. That sort of crap went on with kids.

Jefferson went on to Northwestern for college, and became a national phenomenon in football. I went to one of the games at Northwestern, and a sorority sister of my sister Jane was at the game. Jefferson went wild that day and scored four touchdowns. During one of his runs, this sorority sister jumped up and yelled, "Get him, get him, kill that nigger." After he scored, she sat down and said, "Boy, I sure wish he was on our side!" Those things broke through my upbringing.

In my second year at Calvin College in Grand Rapids, I had to give a speech. The subject was, "Hitler, Mussolini and the NRA." [The NRA was the New Deal's National Recovery Administration.] From then on, I came under President Franklin Roosevelt's spell. I was in the parade for President Herbert Hoover in 1932, and then things began to change.

At Calvin there was a group of seniors, including a writer, Frederick Manfred, who wrote prairie novels and got pretty well accepted nationally. There was also John Huizinga, who wound up in the State Department or CIA. They engaged in a number of escapades to let the conservative faculty know they didn't like their repressive techniques. At that time, you couldn't go to movies or dances. So this group of guys broke into the storage room, took out all the apples and passed them out to the student body. Then the president of the college invited this group to his house on a Sunday evening, and he had put apples all over the place—on tables, chairs, doors, all over. He kept pressing apples on these students. Both Huizinga and Manfred were on the debate team, and took me along on some of their debates. Manfred's real name was Feikema, a Fresian name. The Fresians were one of the most independent groups in Europe. They would fight anyone. I was for the status quo, and they were challenging me!

Mary: In 1933, times were very difficult. My father was a teacher and a dean at Calvin College. He was paid in the fall, when students would come to register, with bushels of apples and tomatoes. They would come by and put them on our front porch. I felt lucky to be able to go to Calvin. I don't think I had to pay tuition, because my father was faculty. The college was about a block from my home. Doug lived a couple of blocks away. We moved in entirely different circles. I was from a middle-class college family. Doug lived in a fairly new and suburban neighborhood. We met in a logic class, which we shouldn't have taken our freshman year. We wound up in a group of students who were pretty serious about their work, but also had a very good time and a lot of adventures, campus escapades, and trips out into the country. My parents weren't very happy about my association with Doug because he wasn't part of the small church group that founded the college. My parents made their peace with that after he graduated from law school and they had time to know him. It was seven years later that we were married.

Doug: At Michigan Law School, we were studying a series of cases about key provisions of the 1935 Wagner Act, which assured workers in private-sector employment the right to organize and bargain collectively. One of the things that was brand new in the law was the duty of employers to bargain in good faith. I developed the idea that if the union presented demands, and the employer said no or only conceded to part of the demands, but didn't claim an inability to pay, that was not bargaining in good faith. Management should have a valid reason for not agreeing to labor's demands, I thought. The day I presented that argument, Mary came to class. After I expounded my theory of what bargaining in good faith really meant, the professor paused and said, "Well, Mr. Hall, I wouldn't say that you are 100 percent wrong!" I might add that my idea has never been adopted by anybody.

You have to understand the background for this. It was 1938, and we were right next door to Flint, Michigan, which had a major General Motors factory. Sit-down strikes were occurring. Every day there were big headlines about this. It was the birth of the labor movement. Frank Murphy was governor of Michigan. In those days, it was pretty hard for a Democrat like Frank to get elected. That was the heyday of John L. Lewis. He had just formed the CIO [Congress of Industrial Organizations], and they put all of their energy behind organizing the auto plants. Walter Reuther and that whole generation of union organizers were emerging. Lewis had a long history in the AFL [American Federation of Labor], and several times he left the AFL and was independent, and then he formed the CIO. One of the times he left the AFL, Lewis gave a speech in which he said, "Gentlemen, I have shared an office on the same corridor with William Green, president of the AFL, for twenty years. I have examined his mind thoroughly. Gentleman I give you my word...there is nothing there!"

At the peak of the sit-down strikes, there was pressure on Governor Murphy to call out the National Guard. The governor was in the hospital with some sort of illness, and about to call out the guard. The story is that Lewis went to visit him in the hospital. Lewis said, "Governor, if you call out the Guard, I will appear in the windows facing heaven. We will open the windows, and I will stand up and bear my breasts and when your troops shoot, I will be the first to fall. When I fall, Frank, you will hear your brother say, 'Frank, have you done the right thing?'" Frank's brother had been shot by the "black and tans" of the British army in Ireland. Murphy did not call out the Guard!

Mary: Doug and I get so emotional about this because we were two kids in our early twenties, out of conservative backgrounds, ultra-Republican and in my case also ultra-academic and religious, never having been exposed to anything that was violent, rebellious, or political. But suddenly, this world all around us is filled with radicalism and progressivism, and the labor movement is opening up before us, and we're trying to decide what to do with our lives.

Doug: In my second year in law school, I had a course in equity. Those were the days when American and English law still had a division between the law and equity. The law side came down from the English monarchs. That was the hard-boiled political and governmental approach. Things got so bad under the monarchs that the English theorists and practicing barristers started to develop equity, which was a way to temper the strict, harsh legal doctrines. In those days, Michigan Law School had that dichotomy. You got your law courses, property, contracts, torts, and criminal law. Then "equity" developed a set of principles to ameliorate that which was thought to be too harsh. Michigan followed the case method of teaching, where professors would use cases from the Supreme Court and federal courts to illustrate principles of law. Right in the middle of the equity course, we had an 1898 case from the Massachusetts supreme judicial court. Oliver Wendell Holmes was on that court. The employees of the Boston Gas Company organized a union, and the gas company took them to court to stop them, on the basis that organizing that union was a criminal conspiracy. It was an eight-to-one decision, with Holmes dissenting. Studying this was almost a religious experience for me. I can still feel the excitement I got out of reading Holmes's dissent. One of his virtues was that he could distill ideas and concepts down to very simple, basic formulations. His dissent stated a very simple principle: "If capital can combine for its advantage, then there is no constitutional reason why labor cannot combine!" That decision came in 1898, and it was 1938 when it had so much impact on me!

Mary: There was never any consideration that I would not follow my parents' lead, go to college and become a teacher. I finished Calvin College, and at that time they were just starting a new Michigan State scholarship program, giving students at colleges a chance to win a full scholarship to the university. I won that, and could go on and get a degree in English literature and be on the campus at Ann Arbor where Doug was in law school. That was 1937. That was a very exciting year for me. For the first time, I lived in a larger and more diverse community than the small one I knew. We spent every Sunday walking in the arboretum, talking about what was going on in the larger world, and what would later become our life.

Until then we had not thought much about the changes within ourselves, and career choices. We had thought that Doug might go into practice with his dad. His father had never taken a partner. There were lots of qualified young attorneys in his office, but no one was eligible to be a partner, because the position was being held for Doug. Doug got to law school, and his big decision was, "How do I deal with this? I can't do that." It was clear that Doug couldn't say yes to Clare J. But his mother had died by then, and his father depended on him. There were lots and lots of unresolved issues there. We came to Minnesota in 1939. Doug passed the bar here in Minnesota just before we were married that September.

Doug: Clare J. was a real stand-up guy. He had one question when I told him I wanted to go into labor law: "Do you really believe that you can accomplish something that way?" I said Yes, and that was the end of it. There was no recrimination or anything. I later went to Chicago, St. Louis, Cleveland, Detroit, and Minneapolis to interview for my first law job. One of my aunts knew a man who was a general counsel for the National Labor Relations Board, and I talked to him about coming into labor law. I went to see one of the general counsels for the auto workers in Detroit and other labor counsels in the other cities. I came to Minneapolis because of my friend Fred Feikema. He worked then for the *Minneapolis Journal* as a sportswriter. He had just gone through the first KSTP strike in 1937 or 1938. He knew the key figures in labor law in the CIO, including Ralph Helstein, a lawyer who had been involved in the early days of the CIO. About a year before I came to Minneapolis, the CIO had organized Minneapolis Moline, a farm implement company, and that was a big start for labor. Ralph needed an assistant, but he didn't have any money, so for the first six months I didn't get a paycheck. The name of the firm was "Helstein and Hall."

Mary: Ralph Helstein was the son-in-law of Arthur and Fanny Brin. Fanny was the first UN chairperson in Minnesota and a founder of the United Nations movement who worked with Eleanor Roosevelt. Her daughter Rachel was married to Ralph and they became our best friends and mentors in Minneapolis. Fanny Brin was known as "the patron saint" of peace-loving people.

Doug: Helstein and Hall was located at 353 Midland Bank Building in downtown Minneapolis. That was 1939. We were living on Kenwood Parkway. Hitler had gone into Poland. Our law practice and major base was local unions, mainly with the CIO but some with the AFL. We did a lot with the hotel and restaurant workers. The CIO was more of the metal manufacturing workers, and AFL was clusters of service organizations, like the restaurant workers. In 1940, we went to the state CIO convention in Austin. One of the great contributions that Helstein made was that he negotiated the first guaranteed annual wage contract with George Hormel, the Austin meatpacker. That was our first paycheck.

We got two new contracts, the Hormel local and another catch-all union that included restaurants and retail clerks. The Hormel local paid us $25 per month. By 1942, Ralph had been hired by the packinghouse workers' organizing committee, and he went to Chicago. That union was right in the middle of the left/right split of the CIO. This was at the same time as the split between the Trotskyites and the Leninists in the Communist Party. Ralph was in the middle of all that, and he told them, "You can believe what you want, but you've got to organize!" He was a close friend of Saul Alinsky of the "Back of the Yards" movement who organized the packinghouse workers in Chicago. The racial and ethnic struggles of that period were mirrored in this packinghouse struggle. Ralph went to live there, and I took over the partnership in 1942.

We organized the Honeywell workers in 1941. That was a skilled union of tool and die makers. We were successful against management, the Sweatts, (sons of company founder W.R. Sweatt) and George Du Toit. That involved the National Labor Relations Board out of Washington D.C. This guy, a hearing examiner, comes in wearing a white linen suit. We didn't even know what white linen was! I think it was in August. The hearing lasted weeks. People testified as to how they had been pushed around by management. This was in the tradition of the truck drivers' strike and conflict, which had happened in 1934.

In 1942, the firm grew. Wyman Smith came in, and became

an expert on municipal law. The suburbs—Coon Rapids, Fridley and Blaine—were expanding rapidly. There was a big lawsuit over the incorporation of Fridley. Jack Hawley, the owner of Northern Pump, was opposed to incorporation. This was a good source of fees for the firm. Then George Hedlund came in, and he also did some municipal work in the Osseo area.

There were several others added to the firm, and we were quite diverse, representing different constituencies. Wyman was a New England Unitarian from Vermont. George was a Scandinavian from Minnesota. Lenny Juster was active in the new St. Louis Park Jewish community. Tommy Forsberg later became a judge. There was also one of Fred Feikema's younger brothers, Henry Feikema. They were a lot of bright, up-and-coming people, and they were very much interested in success. They also had a strong social philosophy. Each of us had a little different slant on life. It was quite a group.

Mary: When Doug was just getting started with Ralph in the law firm, the Spanish Civil War was being fought. This was one of the roots of our radicalism. We mentioned Fanny Brin, who was not a social radical. Her husband Arthur was from a conservative old Jewish family on Lake of the Isles in Minneapolis. Fanny taught a social change class for middle-aged Jewish women, many of them influential behind-the-scenes movers and shakers. In the evenings, there were occasionally suppers where community issues were discussed. Fanny's brother, Mose Barron, who practiced medicine at Mount Sinai, his wife Leah, Bishop James Shannon, Max Seham and Lisl his wife, and Major Moisel all participated. It was Jews, Catholics, and Protestants coming together to discuss current events. These people greatly influenced our later social involvement. I remember sitting on the floor at these wonderful gatherings. Dinner would be served very late, so everyone was quite mellow by that time, and the food was incredible. Some of these events were fundraisers for the Spanish Civil War. People were not afraid to say that this was an anti-fascist meeting, which was a risky thing to do in the early days. Even the Catholic Church supported the Spanish government.

Doug and Mary had five children over ten years. They joked that they were all almost two-and-one-half years apart, and that the spacing was not all that intentional. When their fifth child was born, Doug was counsel for Planned Parenthood. Mary said they would refer to Doug as "The Counsel for the League for Unplanned Parenthood!" Their daughter Kathy was born in 1941, Douglas in January 1944, Margaret (Missy) in 1946, Becky in 1948 and Claire in 1951. All of their kids attended public schools, although son Doug attended Blake for a couple of years, and all graduated from the laboratory schools at the University of Minnesota. They were taught to think for themselves. One of the Halls' great virtues was their respect for their children's right to disagree with their strong liberal philosophy.

Doug: Thinking of Eisenhower always reminds us of our son Doug. When Ike ran against Adlai Stevenson in 1952, we had six Stevenson stickers and one Eisenhower on the back of that station wagon! We had always told our kids that everyone could develop his or her own opinions. Some of our friends went out of their minds over that. They said, "You don't have to do that. It's your car, and he's got no right to do something that you're against." It appalled them that we took him downtown to buy Eisenhower stickers!

My sister Jane was a year and a half older than I was. We had a very good relationship. On politics, we had a great division. She went to the grave thinking Richard Nixon was the greatest thing that ever happened. Jane married an engineer for U.S. Rubber. He was involved in the development of tires for ore carriers in taconite mines. He was very conservative. Eventually Barbara, their daughter, took teacher training, got her degree, and was teaching in Monroe, Michigan. Then she got active in the teacher's union, held local offices, and went to several federation conventions. One of them was here in St. Paul, and we discovered this niece that came from a conservative background, and she was in tune with us philosophically all the way.

While Doug was establishing his law practice, Mary earned her PhD. She taught at the University of Minnesota from 1958 to 1977, becoming a full professor. She trained doctorate-level school psychologists in clinical, child, or educational psychology. She had appointments in all three fields. By 1971, when Children's Hospital opened, she was asked to come on as its chief of psychology. She accepted, and also amazingly continued as a professor at the university.

Doug: In 1968, I was involved in a couple of large pro-bono social justice cases. My partners concluded that they could no longer support me, since I wasn't bringing in any fee income. The Black movement and the Indian movement and to a lesser extent the Hispanic movement were all boiling up in the 1950s and 1960s. I got so swept up in them that I wasn't producing much revenue in the law business. I was the senior partner at the time. The other partners were not embarrassed by my work. It was purely a business and financial decision. I wasn't carrying my share of the load, so they asked me to leave.

By 1969 I was working out of The Way, a not-for-profit neighborhood organization working with youth. The Way was formed on the near North Side of Minneapolis in August 1966, after an event that exposed the anger and frustration of young black men who felt shut out of the system. The Way's purpose was to try to provide a more productive outlet for their energy. Early supporters had been business leaders Ray Plank of Apache Corp., Roger Hale from Tennant Corp., and Louise Walker McCannel, active in the arts and one of the heirs of the T.B. Walker timber fortune.

The Way was often in conflict with the Minneapolis police department, and was involved in some of its most important criminal cases. One of the cases resulted from a street celebration where the police were called, someone got shot, and there were a number of arrests. Someone had shouted, "Death to the blue-eyed bastards." It was a gang member out of Chicago. One of the people arrested was the assistant director of The Way, Joe Buckhalton. This turned out to be a test case for the police and The Way. The court room was packed with young people from The Way. It was one of those cases where the accused hadn't been involved in criminal activity. Buckhalton was there, but he was trying to keep things calm.

The trial was interesting from a number of perspectives. Then, all cases were in Municipal Court the first time around. If you were found guilty, the case went to District Court. By the luck of the draw, the judge was Neil Riley. Neil was a real piece of work. He started out making it clear to our side that we were going to have a chance to be heard. He wasn't going to use any technical reasons to keep the situation from being presented. We wanted to show what this black power, Black Panther thing was really like. We had an expert witness, Arnold Rose from the University of Minnesota's Department of Sociology. He testified at one point that of the whole range of participants in the black movement, the Black Panthers represented a "Puritan strain." Riley leaned toward Rose from the bench and said, "Would you come again with that, professor?" Buckhalton was found not guilty. This happened just before the Legal Rights Center was started, and in terms of fees, it was all pro-bono.

Right then, a significant South Dakota murder case came up. Thomas James Whitehawk, an Indian, was charged with two counts of first-degree murder and rape. It was in Vermillion, South Dakota. He had been represented by a public defender who had almost no experience. The man pleaded guilty and was sentenced to die in the electric chair. He was a very bright young man who had attended Shattuck School in Faribault, Minnesota. The Episcopal Church had taken him in and sent him to Shattuck. There was an alleged assault of some sort by this handsome, promising young man, who had been a star athlete and a war hero. Then suddenly there is this tremendous accusation of rape and double murder, before he completed his first year at the University of South Dakota. Community activists Ron Labertus and Jerry Vizenor came to his defense. Jerry Vizenor was at the University of Minnesota in Native American studies, and was a columnist for the *Minneapolis Tribune*. He was one of the first activists in the Indian community. When Vizenor heard about the death penalty, he went ballistic. They asked me to help.

We concentrated first on getting the death penalty removed. I contacted Cotter Hirschberg, who had been in our class in college. After graduation, Cotter went on to be a psychiatrist, and became a department head at the Menninger Clinic. We contacted him after not seeing him for forty or so years. The group in college had been very close, and those friendships really lasted. I called Cotter and went to Topeka, and he introduced me to the chief forensic psychiatrist there. He came to South Dakota, reviewed all the medical reports, extensively interviewed Tom, and came to the conclusion that Tom had had a "dis-associative episode." On the basis of this report we brought the case to the pardon board. This required three days of hearings in Pierre. You can imagine what the pardon board looked like in South Dakota in the 1960s. The Indian community, especially the young people, really rallied to the cause over the death penalty. The Episcopal Church was involved. The bishop was a fearless guy and gave his full support. So we were able to generate a good deal of favorable public opinion. We made a presentation based on the general level of treatment of Indians in South Dakota, especially in the criminal justice system.

The board eventually removed the death penalty, and then it was life without parole. It was a unanimous vote, including one Indian member. He was a real sellout. There was a Catholic sister who visited Tom regularly in prison. She helped him get college credits in courses like Hebrew and ancient history. He was a real student.

In time a court hearing was held attacking the validity of the original conviction. They had talked him into a confession without an attorney present. We lost in the trial court, and there was a question of appealing. There was no one to support the appeal. We were trying to develop a case before the board to overturn the life sentence. There was a lot of shadowy stuff going on, clerical people coming into the prison for the hearing and then going into back rooms to talk with the parole board itself. To my own satisfaction later, I learned that the Episcopal apparatus, separate and apart from the bishop, had made a deal. They would agree to set aside the death penalty, but Whitehawk was never to get out of prison!

The conviction was in 1968, and the pardon from the death penalty was in 1971. Governor Frank Farrar made a balanced statement at the time of the commutation of the death penalty, but then Farrar turned against us with a vicious attack on Whitehawk. Governor Bill Janklow implied later that he might consider parole, but then he turned against us, saying Tom would be a danger to himself and the public if released. One of Tom's accomplishments was to challenge the censorship of prison mail. He took that on in court and won. Then a young Indian Tom met in prison was paroled and later charged with murder. Tom took that on as a legal assistant, and one of the things he advocated was giving the man a lie detector test. The public defender would not support that, and the man was convicted. Tom kept after that case, and finally got the attention of somebody else in the public defender system. They appealed that conviction, were successful and got the man released. Tom was the moving force, as well as being a very effective witness. The only real pay I got after I left the firm was for the Whitehawk case. I think the diocese raised $25,000.

We started thinking about what came to be The Legal Rights Center in 1968. We spent a couple of years going after logical sources of funding, but had no success. Then Peter Dorsey came along. He had been doing some work with Gwen and Syl Davis, the founders of The Way. He liked the idea of the Center, and called together ten of the leading law firms—Dorsey; Robins, Davis and Lyons; Leonard, Street and Deinard; Lindquist and Vennum; and others. Faegre and Benson came along later. We presented our mission statement, which required that a majority of the board always be from the community. The law firms wanted the board to be made up of lawyers, and a separate advisory board to represent the community. Ever heard of that before? The second problem was the community workers. The lawyers thought they should be people from the law firms. The idea of community workers came from Syl and Gwen Davis, Willie Mae Dixon, and others in the community. Willie Mae was a powerful figure. At that time, there was a lot of agitation on the national level saying that law school graduates should have a chance to do some community service. I was making no headway until Peter Dorsey said, "Gentlemen, these people have a problem, and they have a solution. They are not interested in your ideas or my ideas. You and I are here because we represent money!"

He raised $70,000 and we got started! St. Peter! We started above the Flame Café on Franklin Avenue. It was very important to the Indian community that we be there. Community workers were essential to the process. One reason was that the public defender was not trusted by the communities of color. Bill Kennedy, then Hennepin County's chief public defender, was viewed as an elitist. Our philosophy was that the client makes the decision; the lawyer never makes the decision for the client. This was agreed upon through many hours of meetings.

Our principle of having the client make the decision came from this experience: In one of my South Dakota cases, a young man was accused of homicide. He was drinking with his buddy, and a gun went off and killed someone. During the jury selection process, we always sat down and told the client what his role should be. We had picked eight or nine jurors, and we got to the tenth, who was a bird colonel in the military. I would normally have issued a peremptory challenge and had him dismissed. The client disagreed. He said, "I got two reasons. First, he is a military man, and he has been around guns all his life, and he knows accidents happen. Second, I served in Vietnam, and the colonel will respect that." So we went with that jury, and they found him not guilty! He gave me one of his eagle feathers. That was all during the Vietnam war. Boy, many of my clients were upset with my being against that war. You see, many of these young blacks and Native Americans had gotten their first start and first sense of self respect in the military. In the military, they got the same treatment as the white man, and that was so important.

When the Legal Rights Center got started, Jim Krieger and

Dave Murrin were the first lawyers hired. All three of us lawyers were white. Syl Davis was a social worker and Gwen was a frustrated lawyer and educator. They represented the community, doing the community's work in a law firm. Clyde and Peggy Bellecourt similarly were totally grounded in the community. Pam Alexander and Mike Davis were hired later. The notion of running this law firm like you run a family came out of the heritage of the black and Indian communities, and later the Hispanics. Family is key in those communities. There was such a burning resentment among the activists of those communities that they were not part of the decision-making process, that we required full participation from all of the players. We had some crises in the center over the feeling that decisions should be made only with full consensus. The two people who were most instrumental in working things out were Willie Mae Dixon and Mary Jane Wilson. Those two minority women, one Black, one Native American, virtually held the center together.

We had advertised at the law school and in the journal "Finance and Commerce" for lawyers when Krieger and Murrin applied. One of the sad things was an interview with a young black lawyer and his wife from Chicago. I always started out the interview explaining that the cases were referred to the staff attorney by the community worker, and that the community worker was a key part of the process. This young fellow could not accept that. He said, "I know the law, and I know what's best for these people." So we went back through the whole process again, and he didn't change his mind. Finally, the entire staff got up and walked away from him!

Krieger and Murrin had some experience, but no real felony experience. The community workers were a great source of strength for them. It was harder for Krieger. His father was a beer distributor, and he had worked at the Wilson plant at Albert Lea. He never forgot the Wilson experience. Krieger got more and more radical at the Legal Rights Center. Then he later went to the public defenders' office and did a lot of training and really moved them forward. Murrin was a great systems guy, and really believed in getting the legal system straightened out. He was not as radical as Krieger. In those days, the jobs paid very little, probably less than $20,000 per year.

For the Indian community, a key case there happened at "The Corral," an Indian bar on Franklin near Bloomington Avenue. The only reason anyone went there was to get drunk. I used to hate to have to go in there. The police department had a practice of going there on Saturday night, backing the paddy wagon up to the door, and just shoving people in. Four of the men arrested were AIM guys, young men from Leech Lake and South Dakota. Before the police put them in the paddy wagon, they used to handcuff them and chain them to lamp posts. Then on the way up to the jail, they would rough them up a bit. These four young men, with Clyde Bellecourt assisting, decided that they wanted to stand trial. Again, we drew Neil Riley as the judge. I think we tried it for well over a day.

One of the things we tried to do in Municipal Court was to make the trial function like a District Court case. The system was to fill up the bull pen, and then bring all the accused before the judge at once. Justice was usually dispensed quickly. But we insisted that lawyers sit at the counsel table, that a witness stand be used, and that it run like a court. We were cutting into the spare time of the judge and the city attorney. We laid out how these guys had been victimized. Riley found them not guilty on all six charges against each of them, except one, and that was profanity in public! In those days, there was a law against profanity in public. Riley fined each of them $25 and suspended the sentence! Clyde and the people at AIM took the message to Franklin Avenue: "We can't guarantee you will be acquitted, but we can guarantee you that we will put up a fight." That diffused the tension on the street. So the real message was, "If you are right, you have a chance." This case and The Way case established my credibility in the black and Native American communities, and gave impetus to the founding of The Legal Rights Center.

Mary: Doug had previously had a beautiful large office, with a magnificent huge oil painting by Sid Fossum that now hangs in the Minnesota Historical Society. It's a painting of a union organizing committee called the Workers Alliance. There are some real characters in the painting, like Meridel LeSueur and an Irish immigrant organizer. It's a marvelous painting, perhaps the best of Fossum's work. Sid was on the WPA arts project and he was a prolific producer. There was a misunderstanding over some work related issue and they charged Sid with WPA fraud. The U.S. attorney at that time was Victor Anderson, a "red baiter" from hell, and he was determined to get this strong labor activist artist. Doug defended Sid, won the case, and this marvelous large painting was his pay. The painting stayed in Doug's office after he was forced to leave. Wyman Smith knew its value, and took care of it. Later when Wyman retired, he returned it to Doug, and the two of them presented it to the Historical Society, where it is part of a large Fossum exhibit.

Mary played a key role in one of the most significant and precedent-setting lawsuits that ever impacted the University of Minnesota, the Rajender pay equity case.

Mary: Dr. Shyamala Rajender was a woman chemistry professor who had never been approved for tenure. She started a suit against the university. The first place it would go at the university was a three-person faculty senate committee. I was one of the members; one other was Donald Gillmor from the journalism faculty, whose specialty was journalism law. We held long and very intense hearings. Gillmor and I were the two that voted in favor of giving her the right to legal appeal. The case went to federal court under Judge Miles Lord. She was granted tenure. It made history in terms of women's rights with respect to equality in compensation in the employment field. The University's system had been that tenure was granted on a basis of the faculty's recommendation, but final word rested with the chairman of the department. After the Rajender case an appeal process was permanently put in place, through the faculty senate. I was made chair of an all-university committee on human rights in areas of faculty/administration relationships.

Doug: It's the work of the Legal Right Center that I am most proud of. We broke the barrier between the system and the community, and enabled the community to believe that if they did use the system correctly, they could have an influence on the system. We raised feelings of pride in the Indian and other communities that you could make people listen to you. We had a real impact. Some of that has dissipated and washed away, because of reactionary responses like what former Attorney General John Ashcroft has done. It's just awful. I think our loss has been that many people in the communities have lost interest in some of these issues.

In a number of ways, within Mary's area and mine, we took some of our experiences and what we learned into the peace movement, the women's movement, and the restorative justice movement. I'm pleased that the restorative justice movement is growing. I have been quite interested in our own reactions to the peace movement. We have gotten caught up in the spirit of the thing, like we got caught up in the labor movement, the women's movement, and the civil rights movement. Part of the excitement of that is being in a very conservative community, one that is not too issues-oriented, and to see it grow here. Our first vigil here in Wabasha under the bridge was in March 2003 regarding the Iraq war. One of the activists who organized the vigil said, "If we get four people, I will be really pleased." We got 60 people! So at ages 87 and 88, we are still doing vigils. We were about 24 or so when we demonstrated for the first time at Honeywell. But the feeling it gives you is the same. You go to these meetings and someone says, "I don't really understand how democracy is supposed to work," and you can show them that it really is built from the ground up, bit by bit. It really grabs ahold of you. I have been amazed.

Doug and Mary Hall helping to lead a peace vigil under a Wabasha Bridge as they approached their nineties make an inspiring picture, to say the least. Doug had a smile that went on forever as he described his latter-day activism. His joy and passion were infectious, and live on in those he inspired. Doug Hall's funeral took place in Wabasha on November 14, 2004, in the St. Felix school gymnasium. The chairs were arranged in circles with all of the communities of color represented. The tributes went on and on amid drumming, chanting, singing, and offerings from the various ethnic groups represented. Near the end, a gentleman from Rochester, MN, who sat next to me, Charles Wolsky, rose to speak. He said, "I was the prosecutor on the Thomas Whitehawk case in South Dakota. While Doug Hall and I were on opposing sides of that case, I must say that I have never been in the presence of a more principled, fair-minded, and dedicated man. I will miss his humanity and his great civic leadership."

HUSSEIN SAMATAR

*H*ome is where the heart is, and this is our home. When the plane touches down at the airport, I know I have come home. We feel we have been richly blessed, coming from the refugee camps to Minneapolis.

– Hussein Samatar, May 2006

Hussein Samatar is a veritable advertisement for what is best about the United States. We visited on a beautiful May morning in 2006 at his offices in the Cedar Riverside area, far from the civil war and strife that plagues Somalia, his native land. He speaks with incredible appreciation for the opportunities that have come to him and his family since they arrived in Minnesota. There is sadness in his tone as he relates the story of his native country's collapse after a coup that replaced a duly elected government. His dreams and educational preparation to be an economist for the Somali central bank were shattered his first day on the job. Hussein candidly expresses how emotionally difficult it was for him to accept leaving his native land forever. But his calmness today attests to the fact that he has achieved acceptance, and moved on.

There is a fast pace to his remarks, as if he cannot wait to get to the part where he and his wife start their new life in Minnesota. It is apparent as he speaks that the loss of Somalia's elected government to a dictatorship shocked him, and sensitized him to the gift of democracy, with its opportunity for civic engagement. Hussein is like a child with a new toy as he expresses his wonder at this new phenomenon in his life—the non-profit organization. There is durability about Hussein that will serve him well through any future hardship, and an appreciation for a free society that bodes well for our community in the years ahead.

Hussein founded the African Development Center, formed in 2003 to assist African immigrants and refugees in achieving economic security. It recognizes that most of the 130,000 African immigrants and refugees in the Twin Cities arrived less than a generation ago. ADC helps these new residents overcome language, cultural, and religious barriers that inhibit economic self-sufficiency. The Center "sees a future in which Africans own homes and businesses at rates comparable to Minnesota natives, and reap the personal, political and communal benefits that come with hard-earned economic stability."

Hussein's life is grounded in the discipline and love provided by his mother and the example of a well-managed professional career from his father. That's where his story began:

I grew up in a very small city in the south of Somalia, called Kismayo. People may have heard of Mogadishu, the capital, but our town was much smaller and further south. We had a beautiful beach on the ocean, and I used to go there every afternoon after school to play soccer before going home to do homework, have dinner, and go to sleep. I was born in 1968. That year was a year of great turmoil in Somalia. The president who had been elected by the people was killed that year. He was shot dead. After about one year, the military took over. Up until that period we had a history of peaceful elections. Somalia had been the first African nation to have a sitting president defeated in an election. Unfortunately, his duly elected successor was then assassinated.

While I was growing up, the whole economic system of the country was aligned with the Soviet Union. This same pattern of alignment with communism and socialism was also going on in Tanzania, Ethiopia, and several other countries. However, Somalis by nature are not cut out for a socialistic system. They are nomads who travel and trade goods for a living. The marketplace, where goods are bought and sold, is ingrained in Somali culture. When I showed up for school in 1974, the Somali language had just been written for the first time. For many years, it had only been a spoken language. The new written language had a Latin base, not an Arabic one. So we were the first generation to come to school and learn Somali as a written language.

My father was a police officer. He was a high-ranking member of the force who traveled the country running and leading different police headquarters. He was not military, as the civilian police were entirely separate.

My mother stayed home as I was growing up, and I think that was what made us a very stable family. I was the youngest of five children. My mom was an extremely intelligent human being, even though she never had the opportunity to go to school. She was married when she was 19, and had her first child when she was 20. She ran the household, taking care of her children without any of the appliances we take for granted today. She would get the news in many languages over the radio, and also at the market that she walked to every day where she socialized with other women. Mind you, the climate we lived in was extremely hot, so you had to conserve your energy. It was essential to have a rest period in the middle of the day. We always ate three good meals a day at home.

Later, at the age of 26, my mother went back to school, learned Somali and Italian, and signed up for adult basic education classes. This was in an environment where women were expected to stay at home. Because my father traveled a lot, my mother was the one who came to every parent-teacher conference. She would ask the teacher, "What is he learning?" "What is he not learning?" and "Does he have a positive attitude toward life?" She would ask if I was a trouble-maker or was making noise. This happened every three months. We never had a library, or such a thing as the Internet. Somehow my mother was always able to obtain books from friends or at the market. I never lacked fascinating things to read about.

We children were given a choice of schools, expected to do our homework, help out around the home and do the very best that we could. We always knew that we were part of a global system, and only knowing one language was not going to cut it. In our K-12 system, we were required to know four languages. Of course, the first was Somali; next, Arabic, because we were a Muslim country; then we had English, and finally Italian, because Italy had colonized the southern part of our country. The English had been in the north, and the French also had a few settlements.

We were aware of what was going on in the world, despite the fact that we never traveled and had no computers. There was enough community interaction so that news traveled relatively fast. Also, when I was growing up, it was extremely difficult to participate in the political system. Civic engagement was not possible. We lived under a very authoritarian dictatorship. Anyone who tried to speak out was either detained or killed. This was going on all through the 1970s and 1980s. This was very detrimental to the development of Somalia. I never took this authoritarian style for granted, because my father had grown up in more democratic times, and we learned from him.

After finishing grade school, middle school, and high school, we had two years of national service. Then I was very lucky, and was able to get in to the Somali National University in Mogadishu. It was the only university in our country. I was lucky because that year, eleven-thousand students graduated from high school and the university only admitted one thousand. This was 1987, and the lack of university capacity was the result of years of stagnation by the government, which virtually did no planning. They talked a good game, but all during my growing-up years, the country basically stood still in terms of development. I realized then how lucky and privileged I was to be able to get an education and go on to the university. We were paying no tuition, as the government paid our way in full. I then went on to study economics and graduated with a BA in economics in 1991. I accepted a job doing economic analysis and research for the Somali central bank. The future looked bright.

But things were to change fast for Hussein and his generation, the so-called "lost generation" of Somalia. His experience illustrates how easily events beyond one's control can alter one's course.

Four days after I graduated, the civil war began. That was December 30, 1990. I was never able to work after that. The civil war brought the collapse of all the institutions—the government, schools, hospitals, banks, especially in the southern part of the country. It was a very strong group that got together to overthrow the elected government. When they were successful after two years of fighting, they had no plan for actually running the country. The situation was further confused by strong tribal loyalties, which made it difficult to resolve the conflict. President George H. W. Bush got involved in 1992, sending food and military support in an attempt to stabilize the situation, but the rivalries were too strong, and the U.S. pulled out.

There was gunfire and shelling going on all over the place. I made my way from the university back to our home in Kismayo. My mother had passed away in 1982 and my father in 1986. After I returned home, I soon left for Mombassa, Kenya.

Here I was, a college graduate in my early twenties, extremely naïve, with no family. My siblings were grown and gone. There was no social network for me to enter. This was when I had to make the most difficult decision of my life. At age 22, after having had all of that fine education and the support of a large family, I told myself that my new home would have to be wherever I landed. There was no way I could ever return to Somalia. I also knew that I had to turn my back on my Somali tribal division. I would have to embrace the culture of the land I settled in, or I would not survive. This was extremely difficult for me, but once I made the decision, there was no turning back. Survival was the key, and that did not permit time for nostalgia. When you visit a country as a tourist and study the culture, that's one thing, but when you are born there and must leave, it is quite another. It was very, very difficult.

Another thing had a lasting impact on me. Life is so fragile. We were eleven days on the boat from Kismayo to Mombassa. There were many mothers with children, and not enough food or water to go around. It became very clear to me how important it is in a society to have systems set up that offer assistance to those who need help.

The second day after we arrived on shore, I went to the man, a Belgian, who was in charge of the United Nations refugee camp. I told him that I was highly educated, spoke four languages, but had never worked a day in my life. I said, I think I can be of help to you! He asked me my name and where I was from. He then asked why I thought I could be of help to him. I said, because I speak Somali and you can't communicate with the Somali refugees. We then talked for half an hour, and he told me that he would find something for me to do. The next day, I went to work forming a data base and taking down the names of all of the displaced people in the camp and where they were from. One of the main goals was to reunite families that had become separated. This was the first job of my working career. The next week I mentioned to the manager that I appreciated having food and a place to sleep, but what about getting paid for my work? We made an arrangement, and I did that work for him one year. It involved trying to provide everything a human being needs to survive. Many refugees came with physical and emotional problems, and we did the best we could to help each family. It was a very large camp with about fifty-thousand people. I never imagined when I received my B.A. degree in economics that I would become a social worker. I loved helping people find their friends and relatives.

There were four countries that stepped up and said that they could help resettle some refugees, the United States, Australia,

Canada and Sweden. There was a long waiting list, and it was required that you have some contact in the host country. I had no relatives or contacts in any of these countries. One day, one of the UN people approached me and said, "Hussein, have you ever heard of a place called Minneapolis?" He went on to add that it was in a state named Minnesota in the USA, and that more than a thousand Somalis had settled there. I hurried to find a map to see where this small city they talked about was located. I had no sponsor and came to Minnesota seeking asylum and shelter from war.

Soon after my arrival in the Twin Cities, I became involved in community development. I had seen how easy it was to destroy a society and how difficult it was to rebuild after things fall apart. I decided to be a builder.

The culture of the Twin Cities was so different from what I had experienced in Somalia. My first objective was to improve my English. The library became an extremely important resource for me. I had no idea then, of course, that one day I would be appointed to serve on the Minneapolis Library Board. Every day, I was the first person to stand outside the library doors when they opened at 9 a.m. I also attended the University of St. Thomas to further my English skills. The program was free at that time and very helpful.

When I came to Minnesota, the landscape for Somali immigrants was very different than it is today. There were no established English learning programs for Somalis, as there were only about a thousand of us in the Twin Cities at that time. Of course I needed to find a job, so I approached one of the temporary employment agencies. I was well-schooled in accounting and finance. Fortunately, there was a six-month project in trust operations that they tested me for at Norwest Bank [today's Wells Fargo]. I qualified for the job, and went to work for a man named Ted Garrity in March 1996. Things must have gone well, because in June, they told me that I was an extremely hard-working person, and asked me if I would like to stay on in a permanent position. I made many friends who helped me, including Dean Koopman and David Wiese, an alumnus of the Urban Adventure program. David does the CRA [Community Investment Act] work for Wells Fargo. My next job at the bank was in equipment finance and I did that until 1998, when I went back to school to get my MBA at the University of Saint Thomas.

After I received my MBA, I was put in a commercial banking training program at Wells Fargo. I became a business banker, and began the rotation in small business banking. Because of my experience in Somalia, I wanted to find a place where I could make a difference and improve the community. I was assigned to the Wells Fargo Bank at Calhoun Isles, in south Minneapolis. It was at this time that I was also exposed through the Urban Adventure program to community development corporations and how they help revitalize some of the city's most economically challenged neighborhoods. The whole concept of non-profit organizations had not been familiar to me. In 2003, I became a board member of the Neighborhood Development Corporation managed by Mike Temali.

I must thank Hussein for his unsolicited commercial for Urban Adventure. I started this urban education curriculum and experiential learning program after retirement from the investment business in 1996. It seeks to show executives in business how they can be involved in urban economic development in a manner that is beneficial to both their business and the community. Nearly 200 executives have completed Urban Adventure. Mike Temali of the Neighborhood Development Center is one of the presenters in this program, along with other social entrepreneurs such as Joe Errigo, formerly of Common Bond Communities, and Sandra Vargas, president of the Minneapolis Foundation.

By 2003, I had been in the Twin Cities nearly ten years. The African immigrant community had grown, and wanted to be a part of the growing economy of the region. However, there was no organized system available to help them accomplish that. I went to work for Mike Temali, with the understanding that I would work to develop an African American immigrant economic development organization and, if successful, lead it. We were successful, and the new enterprise was called the African Development Center of Minnesota. I became its executive director, and we became the first ethnic immigrant micro-enterprise lender in the state. Our first funding came from the McKnight Foundation and Payne-Lake Community Partners (PLCP), which was then headed by Paul Fate. Later we were supported by the Bush, Bremer, and St. Paul foundations. Today about 25 percent of our budget is fee income, since we charge for many of our services.

To date, we have leveraged more than $8 million of lending since January 2005. We worked closely with Franklin Bank, Wells Fargo, Bremer Bank, and Western Bank to structure loans that work for start-up businesses. We also work closely with the city of Minneapolis, making use of their 2 percent lending program, as well as the CDCs and the Metropolitan Consortium of Community Developers. We have about ten businesses we have assisted in locating in the new Global Market at the old Sears site, with loans of about $25,000 each.

When I speak about leverage, I refer to those lending resources we have to support micro-enterprise loans and technical assistance. For example, we apply for and receive $600,000 from the Minnesota Department of Employment and Economic Development. We leverage that with funds from the Consortium of Neighborhood Developers, the Neighborhood Development Center and private equity. The initial $600,000 is leveraged about two times and funds 45 projects. A second example would be a small business that we believe could do business with a bank if its financial reporting and business plan were in proper order. We provide the technical assistance that helps secure funding from the financial institution. We join the clients as they sit down with the financial institution and help with the review and explanation of the business plan. We have about ten deals that fit this category, with financial requirements that average about $250,000. Some of these are in the new Global

Market at the former Sears site; others are on Lake Street, Cedar Riverside, and Nicollet Mall, with still others on University Avenue in St. Paul. Another project was a gas station that required financing of $750,000. Our largest project involved two businessmen and required financing of $2.1 million. In summary, the leverage comes from the banking community, other CDCs, and the government. This requires that we find partners for every deal, and maintain a solid reputation as we network throughout the community. An example of this is the close relationship we have with Mike Temali and the city of Minneapolis.

We believe that having less does not make someone less of a person than anyone else. Earning a lower standard of living is simply a transition that we are going through. We do not want to have less. We want to have more. The way to do that is through hard work, dedication, and finding out what you do best and doing it. I think that is the bottom line for my people. So coming from a country where many people had less education and a lower standard of living is not so important. It is what you do with what you have that really matters.

I can't help but appreciate how well my parents prepared me for the future, even though I had no idea what lay ahead. My mother had a profound influence on me. With five children and all that there was to do, she could have left me alone, but she didn't. I always knew that she cared. My father used to tell me, "Life is about choices, Hussein. You must be the one to decide what you want to do and become." Because he was so involved in the criminal justice system, he would tell me to avoid getting caught up in negative behavior at all cost. While he was a reformer, he knew that in Somalia, the criminal justice system did not allow second chances. His constant reminder to me was, "Get it right the first time!" He would add that in some cases, people may offer you a second chance, but that you never would know for sure, because first impressions are so powerful in people's minds.

My sisters are all very caring human beings who gave back to their communities. One is a nutritionist, one is a dentist, and the oldest ran the entire hospital system in the city in which I grew up. She died there when people started shelling the hospital. The women in my family made it through high-school and graduate schools, and were able to provide for their own families as well as participate in the community. They knew what leadership was all about.

Some people in this country believe that Muslim women stay in the background. That is not the way it was in those days. All of my family now live outside of Africa. We stay in touch with e-mail and by phone. You can see that we have adapted to many different cultures. Our three children know that they have aunts, uncles, and cousins in many countries.

I can't believe we have now been living here for twelve years, and that life has been so good to us. At age thirty-eight, I have come to love Minneapolis, and we consider it home. I travel in my work attending many conferences in other parts of the country. Home is where the heart is, and this is our home. When the plane touches down at the airport I know I have come home. We feel we have been richly blessed, coming from the refugee camps to Minneapolis.

For the African American Development Center, our plan is to grow and be accountable to our community, so that our people can be a part of the market economy. Assisting new entrepreneurs and helping expand home ownership is central to our mission. If we are to do that, this organization must be run like any successful business, with effective planning and solid management. In addition, we must help in formulating sound public policy, as part of our obligation as citizens. We must participate in the elective process to make sure that our voices become blended with others to make Minnesota's quality of life as good as possible for everyone. I personally love civic engagement, and want to participate in elective politics. If my wife will allow me and if our situation is such that we know our three children's future is secure, I would like to run for public office myself.

Hussein Samatar's incredible escape from war-torn Somalia at the peak of his educational training is a lesson in courage that is only equaled by his appreciation for the United States and his dedication to community service. He is young, and we will benefit immensely from his leadership in the years ahead.

BRENDA ST. GERMAINE

*I had seen Franklin Avenue go up and then down
and then back up again, and it was time to leave. I
had won all the awards and met all the people. I did
a damned good job. I'm proud of what I did. The old
hippie made it. She wasn't supposed to, but she did.*

— Brenda St. Germaine, December 2004

Drive east on Franklin Avenue in Minneapolis from Chicago
Avenue to the Mississippi River, and you see a once-blighted
neighborhood undergoing an amazing positive transformation.
What was once a seemingly never-ending string of bars and deteriorating storefronts has turned into a thriving commercial corridor, hosting a major business incubator, a large shopping center,
a state-of-the-art bakery, a renovated public library, attractive
restaurants, and a host of thriving commercial and social service
facilities.

That change is in large measure the handiwork of the American Indian Business Development Corporation, formed in 1975
and intent on expanding businesses and creating jobs in the Phillips neighborhood on the near south side of Minneapolis.

When Brenda St. Germaine became active in the neighborhood, it was much the same as it had been when I was in high
school in the 1950s—a place respectable people tried not to go

near. But as director of the American Indian Business Development Center, Brenda was about to demonstrate how even such a persistent downward trend line can be reversed.

With her Native American roots, Brenda St. Germaine was the right person at the right time to pioneer the revitalization of economically depressed commercial corridors, reducing crime and creating businesses and jobs along Franklin Avenue, with the support of both the business and foundation communities. In the early 1980s, my wife Anne and I worked with Brenda on various civic projects. She struck me as a no-nonsense, hard-driving woman who did not take no for an answer. When I sat in her office, which was usually filled with clouds of cigarette smoke, I was made aware that time was precious, and I'd better get to the point fast. Her style was, "Cut out the crap and let's get the damned deal done."

It was twenty years later that I called her for this interview. She had moved to a small house just north of Minneapolis and was not in good health. Her mind was sharp on that December day in 2004, but time had taken its toll on her physical well-being. She had kept her sense of humor and playful nature, as she used a water pistol to keep her kitten from jumping on me, the recording device, and the furniture. Her enthusiasm for life had not waned, and her commitment to her community was as deep as ever. Brenda was struggling financially and was recovering from a recent hospitalization that would leave her permanently disabled. But the positive energy in her story kept me on the edge of my chair the entire morning.

I was born in a small town in Wisconsin of about a thousand people, a farming community called Greenwood. I was an only child. My dad was an alcoholic who seldom worked. My mom was a secretary who never missed a day of work until she went into labor with me. My dad was part American Indian, and some of my early childhood was spent on a northern Wisconsin reservation. I remember one time when we were staying at Chief Fleming's house, when I was about five. I went out in the middle of the night to use the outhouse. As I was sitting there, I heard this very loud bear outside growling and pawing the ground. All I could do was sit there until someone woke up and came outside to find me.

My mom took me to Norwegian Church dinners, and my dad took me hunting and fishing. By the time I was fifteen, I had read every book in the town library. I spent a lot of time alone down by the river at the edge of town. I was a very good writer and an artist, and interested in a ton of things that kids my age weren't involved with. Then the Beatles hit Greenwood (and the world) in 1964. My friends and I embraced the '60s mindset of free thinking and individuality. I planned to get out of town when I graduated from high school, since I knew there was more out there and I wanted to find it. I got straight A's and got a full scholarship from the University of Wisconsin. The summer after graduation, at age 17, I headed for the Twin Cities with my friend Pat. Another friend, Marge, had gone a year earlier, so we had a temporary home. I had $40 and my 12-string guitar. We were ready to discover the world. My first memory of the big city was seeing a guy urinating by the Guthrie Theater.

Nobody wanted to hire me at age 17, but I finally got a job at the Art Instruction School because I could type about 800 words a minute! Do you remember the heads on matchbook covers saying "Draw Me" or "You Too Can Be Picasso"? I was there for three months, typing all these applications. It was really boring, but it was a job.

I never did get to college. I was going to hitchhike to California like a lot of kids, but I didn't do that either. I even missed Woodstock. I loved the hippie movement, the changing attitudes, and the emergence of great people. I was a weekend hippie, but totally a working-class girl during the week. I'd traded in my high school clarinet and oboe and bass clarinet for my guitar, so I was actually pretty good at music, and started playing protest songs about Vietnam and other social injustices. By the way, I did get to see the Beatles in person, twice. I marched for Martin Luther King. I believed in his dreams, and mine. I was always for the underdog, and out to change the world—you know, a big-hearted Leo.

I had an apartment above Dudley Riggs' Brave New Workshop on 26th and Hennepin. I played guitar at Dudley Riggs and once at Northrop Auditorium, and I wrote a lot of songs. At Dudley Riggs, they had a big billboard on the roof, and I lived on the top floor. Once after work, I went out onto the roof and sat on the edge, playing the guitar. One of the neighbors saw me and called the police, thinking I was a jumper. The police came rushing up, interrupted my music and hauled me off of the roof.

By day, I was working my way through banks, because that is what I could do. I was good with numbers. Northwestern National Bank of Minneapolis, the old "Weather Ball Bank," hired me when I turned 18. I started as a messenger. Then they put me downstairs in the money room. After about two days it all became just green paper, and not such a big deal. We had to destroy old money that had been recovered from robberies and, in one case, from the Mississippi River. Not a good smell. So I did that for a couple of years. My boss, Arthur, who was quite old, gave me all kinds of hell for my long hair and short skirts, but we ended up really liking each other.

They decided to make me a teller. There were a lot of rules back then. Women couldn't be an installment loan officer; you couldn't smoke at your desk, but the guys could; you couldn't wear pants, and you had to be twenty-one to be a teller. These were stupid rules to me. They finally put me at "walk up" because I was so fast with the money machine. I worked for Northwestern Bank for two years, and quit on my birthday. That started a pattern of working two years at a job and quitting on my birthday, August 15.

Brenda and I were at Northwestern National Bank at the same time, but we never met. It was a time where tradition ruled. Most bankers believed that women couldn't handle a bank's normal service delivery systems, so the fact that Northwestern Bank had a "women's department" was widely advertised. Those were also

the initial days of magnetic ink character recognition on checks. Tabulating was about to be phased out; the advent of the computer was just around the corner.

When Martin Luther King was murdered in April 1968, many of us marched. It was a moment of great social change for the downtown business community, and especially the banks. We marchers for Dr. King came down Marquette Avenue en masse chanting, "Flags at half mast." I must admit being a bit unnerved as we approached Northwestern. The group would stop marching and keep chanting until the person in charge of the flag up on the roof got the word from senior management to lower the flag. I have often wondered what the initial reaction of senior management was when they saw that large group and heard all that noise—but I never asked.

I worked at IDS Mortgage for two years, took some courses at the University of Minnesota, and continued to be a weekend hippie. I was at Marquette Bank and watched when Carl Pohlad met with Jimmy Dean and talked about starting a sausage business. I also led a few female employee protests about wearing pants suits. Guess who won?

At Marquette, there was a really crabby guy who was a mortgage collector. You know, the kind of guy who says, "I'm going to take your children if you don't pay up." Well, he finally quit. They had a stack of those old perforated computer printouts about an inch thick, listing delinquencies. No one wanted that job. I asked the boss to let me try out. I was about twenty-two. The top boys were not excited, to say the least. I was kind of the office joke. But I got my chance.

I would get on the phone as a mortgage collector, and say that I realized times were hard, and they had bills and kids, et cetera. I would say, "Just send me part of your grocery money so I don't have to send this to the attorney, anything to show activity on your account." One guy told me he would give me a payment if I went up in his plane with him. So I did, and he did all these flips and stuff, scared the hell out of me, but I got the mortgage payment of $130. So I did deals with people, and talked nice, and after three months, guess what? The delinquencies dropped from about 40 pages to four! Now the boys weren't laughing anymore, but since they never had had faith in me, I said, "Here's my two-week notice." My feeling was that they didn't deserve me. I was a rebel back then, and believed they should just give people a chance.

My next job was at First Bank Plymouth, on the near North Side, a racially diverse and rapidly changing part of town. This was 1972, and John Warder was the Plymouth branch's president. He liked me, and felt that I should become aware of other Indian people and programs. This ended up being a good thing, but at the time, I didn't care about discovering the Indian community on Franklin Avenue. I also took some good-natured kidding about being part Indian. Some of my co-workers would start doing some drum beating on their desks when an Indian song came over the bank's music system, but I took it well, and we got along fine.

At the time, First Bank did not have any female loan officers because women weren't allowed to test for the position. I told Mr. Warder that I wanted to take the test. I knew I was pretty smart. It's a curse. I went downtown and took the test and passed. I then moved to installment lending. In the year I made installment loans, I only had one bad loan. I would make deals with people, fight for them in the loan committee meetings, and those loans would get repaid and my customers would come through. Then I also got into loan collecting. One guy whose car we tried to repossess drove it into the parking lot and set it on fire. Never a dull moment, and there was no typical day. That was one of my favorite jobs.

One of my boss's customers was an Indian guy named Ralph. Some days when he came in, he would just sit by my desk and watch me work. He ran a chemical dependency program. He asked me one morning if I was part Indian. I said, "Yeah, are you?" It was obvious that he was a full-blooded Native American. He just started laughing and offered me a job as his assistant director. The organization was a state-funded chemical dependency program, the Native

American Council on Chemical Dependency. At that time, none of the statewide chemical dependency centers had Indian counselors, even though their work included training and job placement. I knew nothing about non-profits, grant writing, or fundraising, but I thought banking was a little slow for me, and I wanted something more. Once again, I quit the bank on my birthday, August 15, and joined Ralph. I didn't know that Ralph had an alcohol problem. After a few weeks of working with him, he slipped and got fired. The board of directors decided to keep me and I got a new boss.

Our office was a duplex at 2715 Portland Avenue South, and it was haunted. There were weird sounds and things kept getting moved around. There were six guys in the office. We used to sit around and talk about spiritual things—dreams, Indian history, and many other topics. I felt that I fit right in. I learned that just about everything that had happened to me had happened to them. I saw a lot of part-Indian folks who looked just like me. I was beginning to discover who I was, and getting reacquainted with an Indian community. As part of the job, I got to visit every Indian reservation in the state. It was a great learning job. This agency made a lot of positive changes throughout the state in the field of chemical dependency. But we closed after three years because the funding ran out.

One of the ladies who used to come into Plymouth Bank knew Roger Cook, a vice president at the Federal Reserve Bank, who was Indian. She also was Indian and worked at the state Department of Economic Development. Her name was Charlotte White. (At that time my name was Brenda Freeman. Later it became Draves, and still later St. Germaine. I married Draves twice. Does this ever end??) We were all concerned about the condition of Franklin Avenue and the lack of city interest in its improvement.

This was about 1974. The avenue was run down, with lots of bars, no job opportunities, and no new businesses looking to locate there. In the 1960s when Interstate 35W went through, many wealthy families sold their mansions and moved to the suburbs. Franklin Avenue was a mess from Chicago Avenue to Bloomington Avenue. The freeway made Franklin Avenue an island. Many of the old shops on Franklin closed up. There was Fred, an Italian guy who had a restaurant on Franklin and Chicago. There was a Lerner's clothing store and a jewelry store. Once the freeways came through, all that remained was Gray's Drugstore and Kaplan Brothers Clothing. The only action in the area was by Joe Selvaggio, the director of Project for Pride in Living, who used to pull up to my office in an old Cadillac that had been donated to his agency. Didn't we look strange together?

I don't think those of us who lived in the suburbs at the time anticipated the profound effect that the federal highway program launched by the Eisenhower Administration in the 1950s would have on urban life. While it made the suburbs easily accessible to city residents, it also interrupted the natural flow of life in urban neighborhoods, and tipped some aging neighborhoods into serious decline. For example, on the near North Side of Minneapolis, Interstate 94 separated the residential neighborhoods to the west from the centers of employment to the east along the Mississippi River, harming both. The same was true for the Phillips neighborhood in south Minneapolis as 35W cut south of downtown. Neighborhoods from the University of Minnesota east to St. Paul were dislocated; the Rondo area, St. Paul's African American neighborhood, was especially hard hit. Because it was both cheaper and politically easier to dislodge housing in poorer neighborhoods, lower-income families suffered the most from these changes. Some were forced to relocate; others, to live in a place rendered less desirable by freeway sights and sounds. Traffic patterns were disrupted, forcing many local businesses to close. In many cases, neighborhood leadership fled to the suburbs, creating opportunity for criminal elements to take advantage of a deteriorating economic environment. Franklin Avenue may have been the Twin Cities' most glaring example of the damage a super-highway can do, but it was certainly not the only one.

I remember Charlotte and me sitting in my living room and

dreaming about what we could do. We wrote an analysis of the situation on Franklin Avenue. There was high unemployment, only part-time jobs available, an X-rated theater, few businesses—and all of this only a mile from downtown. The bars were the only action. There was Mr. Arthur's with the bullet holes in the ceiling, the Bear's Den, and the Corral. We decided that we should start a project for job creation. I thought it sounded interesting, and figured I would give it my usual two years, then move on.

We formed a non-profit, the American Indian Business Development Corporation, in 1975. One of the first people we talked with was Bill Messenger, an attorney, who helped us get organized. We decided Franklin Avenue needed a corporate sponsor, so we talked to Honeywell. We thought the area needed a factory. We formed a board, and Roger Cook was the chair. Later I succeeded him. Roger was a tough chair but a great teacher. There was Roger, Bill Messenger, Rick MacArthur, Charlotte, a few others and myself. We all had full-time jobs at the time. Honeywell agreed to commit a significant part of their "five percent of profits" philanthropic formula to the project. We then decided to have a neighborhood meeting, to ask the neighborhood what they wanted. At that time south Minneapolis had the second-largest urban Indian American population in the country.

Roger Cook chaired the meeting at the Indian Center. We provided food, something we felt helped to get people to come. And they came! I took notes. They didn't want a factory or anything like that. They wanted a grocery store, a shoe store, a bookstore, a clothing store, a drug store, and a restaurant. They wanted everything every other normal neighborhood takes for granted. We sat down later and began the design of a shopping center. Eventually the shopping center ran from 12th to 14th Avenues. It took eight years to complete. This project was never supposed to happen, certainly not by a woman-led organization. I wasn't smart enough to know I couldn't do it!

I was elected director of AIBDC in about 1976. At the time I was pregnant, which ended up being a good fundraising tool.

My first office was at the Indian Center, and then in the former Brooks Mansion at 2445 Park Avenue that had been boarded up and bought by an attorney. Mark Dayton, the future U.S. senator, gave us $1,000 to get started, and then we received $10,000 from MEDA, the Metropolitan Economic Development Association. Chuck Poe ran MEDA. That money lasted a year.

We began the initial work on the shopping center. It was just a hellish project! Everything was an uphill struggle. I was fortunate to have super mentors. I was smart, could write well, and got along well with people, but this deal was way beyond my experience. But I learned. I remember being scared to death when I had to speak at meetings such as the Chamber of Commerce and tell our story in front of forty guys. There were rarely any women there. I used to stand in the bathroom until I pulled myself together. These were big men about town, you know, Mr. This and Mr. That! I did a lot of speaking, and after a while, started making friends. But the Franklin story was a very hard sell. Mayor Charles Stenvig and the city council person would not even speak to me. I was definitely the new kid. We found out that we needed some federal EDA [Economic Development Administration] help. They had an office in St. Paul, and were tough to work with. We had to do a feasibility study and prove the area was in need, which we did. They eventually gave us $40,000, and that really started us moving.

We needed to get funding help. I knew very little about funding on a local level. I heard that the Minneapolis Foundation had a reputation for helping organizations get started. I went over to the Foshay Tower and met with Jim Shannon and Tom Beach. This was the winter of 1976, and I was very pregnant. I took the bus over and just looked like hell. They put me under the hot lights and asked me just exactly what it was that I wanted to do. I was scared to death. I tried to explain what economic development meant. The term was generally not understood back then. They knew chemical dependency, health issues, and job skill training, but not economic development. Jim Shannon asked a lot of questions like, "How are you going to get a grocery store to be the anchor?" I didn't have all the answers, but told him that I would find out. We wound up getting a $10,000 grant. Years later at a tribute at St. Thomas, Jim said, "This woman came in and didn't have many answers to our questions. But we concluded that the area needed help, and if anyone was going to get this done, it was going to be Brenda!" A few years later, I would be elected to the Board of Trustees of the Minneapolis Foundation, and chaired the Distribution Committee for eight years. It was a lot different trying to decide how to give money away instead of asking for it.

The city wound up eventually condemning the shopping center property and giving it to us. This was a start for a new Franklin Avenue. I had my child in 1977. I could only use that funding strategy once! Through the Minneapolis Foundation, I was asked to speak at the Itasca Seminar, where I met a variety of people. At the seminar, a man named Bill Humphrey from General Mills came up to me and said, "Would you mind if we funded you?" Are you kidding!! I also met Sharon Sayles Belton, the future mayor, and filled her in on the project. Another national figure I met there was Neal Peirce, a syndicated columnist from Washington D.C.

By 1978 we finally had the land, the architects, the design, and some funding. We couldn't get EDA money until we were 70 percent leased. By then, I had a pretty good board put together. It got up to twenty-four members, which we eventually restructured to twelve. At one time, I picked a board member for every problem I might run into. I had a policeman, a banker, the vice president of real estate for General Mills, a schoolteacher, a minister, several Indian members from the community and so forth. Everything was set, until the city discovered that a main sewer line ran right under our proposed parking area. They said we couldn't build on it, and told us the project was dead. But Jim Heltzer at MCDA [Minneapolis Community Development Agency], the city's economic development office, believed in us and helped. What we wound up finally doing was splitting the project and not building over the sewer line. It seemed that there was always some new problem cropping up.

Eventually things came together, and the organization starting getting recognition. Kellogg Foundation invited me to Detroit, and then sent me to a conference at the Black Feet reservation where I met Buffy St. Marie, a recorded Indian singer. We were getting UDAG grants and CDBG funds. I think I was earning $25,000 or so at the time, after starting at $10,000. I thought I would only be there a couple of years, but the work seemed to never get done. I ended up staying twenty-two years. People ask me why I stayed, and I tell them it was because we weren't finished. The project just kept going and going and going, with one problem after another.

One particular neighborhood group was really tough to work with, but I learned a few tricks. One night at a neighborhood meeting, we needed to get a very critical vote from the group. I knew the group was not going to support our project. I called my friend at an Indian group home and said I needed twenty Indian guys to come to our meeting. I said that they wouldn't have to say a word, but just stand there. The night of that vote, guess what, twenty guys showed up, didn't say anything, and when it came time for a vote, our project was approved. Then my guys walked out and went home. That neighborhood group was eventually de-funded by the city because of lack of diversity in membership.

I kept learning. It had taken me four years to figure out that I wasn't asking executive director Russ Ewald at the McKnight Foundation for enough money. He kept turning me down for $5,000 grants, until Bill Humphrey told me to go in and ask for $20,000 a year for three years. We got approved and Russ said to me, "Well, you finally figured it out." Stanley Tabor, vice president of real estate at General Mills, taught me leasing. Stanley felt that we needed a full-time development firm to help us complete the project, so he set up interviews with local companies. The Wagner Corporation was the second to the last interview, and we hired Lowell Wagner. Lowell was our consultant and held my hand through the process, in addition to running his own firm. He stayed with us for fifteen years. He was the one that helped us bring Bruegger's Bagels to Minneapolis. He also worked to bring in Crown Auto, Payless Shoes, and Country Club food market. Stanley helped me with several leases, including Walgreens. The grocery store was the hardest. We went to Super Valu, Red Owl, and finally Country Club Markets, which said yes. After a ten-minute meeting, they gave us a twenty-year lease. That got us up to the 70 percent lease figure the federal grant required.

Then President Ronald Reagan took office, and he froze all the EDA funds and stopped our project. That was one of the worst days of the project. We immediately went down to City Hall and talked with Mayor Don Fraser about the situation. He brought Jim White from the MCDA into the discussion, along with council member Brian Coyle. Jim said, "I wish someone knew a national reporter." My mind went back to the Itasca Seminar and I remembered my conversations with Neal Peirce. I spoke up, and asked if anyone knew Neal Peirce. They just looked at me. I told them the story and said I would call him, never in a million years thinking he would remember who I was. Well, he did remember, and I told him what was happening to the project. He came here and visited me. He spent two days walking the project with me, seeing homeless people sleeping in boxes and the run-down conditions of the area. He was so impressed with what we were trying to accomplish that he wrote a column in the Washington Post and referred to me as "a scrappy part-Chippewa woman"! The article basically told the story of what Reagan was doing to this poor neighborhood in Minneapolis. He invited some key politicians over for dinner and told them the story, while I went up and down Franklin Avenue collecting petitions. Everyone signed. To make a long story short, Reagan finally agreed to fund eleven projects nationwide, including us. I always wondered who number twelve was.

We were finally on our way and began to build. During the spring, Neal Peirce called me and during the conversation, mentioned his daughter, Andréa. She was on her way to an eastern college and was looking for a summer internship. So in the summer of 1981, she came out and stayed with some family in Minnetonka and worked on Franklin Avenue with me. She just hung around the office and learned all she could. That was really something, that he trusted us to have his daughter work that tough neighborhood with us. We finally opened the center in the fall of 1982, and the night before the groundbreaking, with one hundred and fifty people set to show, we had the blizzard of the century! Have you ever tried to cancel a ground breaking the night before?

Nothing was ever easy, but often, things were funny. One story concerns a bar on Franklin called The Bear's Den. One of the Indian guys on my board, Donny Fairbanks, owned it. He had inherited from the previous owner some stuffed animals—a huge polar bear, moose head, a cougar, foxes, elk horns, and stuffed birds and fish. Helen Cooley, the wife of former Minnetonka mayor and dog kennel operator Bill Cooley, was on our board. We had talked about putting a Burger King in where the bar was. Bill liked the idea, and bought the bar. He then had financial problems, and the bank foreclosed on the bar. I told Bill that if he ever lost the bar, I wanted the animals, because they were part of Franklin Avenue's history. Time passed, then one day Helen called me at 8 a.m. and said the bank was coming in at 2 p.m. and locking the place up. If I wanted the animals, I had to move fast. I said, "What the hell am I going to do?" This was August. I called my snow removal guy, who had a large flatbed trailer, but no workers. Then I went out on Franklin Avenue with $10 bills and hired a group of the locals to help. These folks hung out close by, and we knew them all by name. We went into a bar that had been boarded up for two years. It was like a time warp. Everything was as it originally had been. So here we had six Indian guys loading these huge animals onto the flatbed with pulleys and ropes, and of course some neighbor called the cops, and we had to explain what the deal was. We made quite a sight, riding down Franklin Avenue looking like a float. It was another typical day for me on Franklin.

After we opened the shopping center, I became the manager. I had to learn management, real quick. It was the day before Thanksgiving, and we had this huge blizzard. I hadn't figured out that you needed to contract for snow plowing before it snowed.

After many calls I found a guy to plow, but then I needed sand. I called Helen Cooley, and we went out in the middle of the night with a pickup truck and got enough sand to cover the shopping center parking lot.

After completing the shopping center, we started planning our second project, the business center, in about 1988. When we built that building, I pulled all the animals from the bar out of storage and moved them to our offices, with the big polar bear next to my desk. It was quite a sight. People would come in before a meeting and pet the bear.

The business center, or incubator, went really fast, if you can call four years fast. By then we had established a track record, and we had all the key players lined up. We had to explain what a business incubator was. The concept was not well known. A business incubator is a building offering affordable rent, shared office services, and a hands-on approach to management for new and growing businesses. We wanted office and manufacturing tenants, along with job skill training. We were not sure how to design the interior of the center, or how to split the various space sizes. We had lots of help. It was another learning experience. Once it was up and running, we never had to advertise for space. Word of mouth and public relations did the job. If there was an Indian person in the neighborhood that wanted to start a business, he or she came to us.

We would do the tenants' mail and other office support. We brought consultants in and helped them shape their business plans. As it turned out, Banner Creations was one of our first tenants. In the beginning, the owner, Nora Norby, only had an assistant with a sewing machine. Before long, she took up nearly half the space in the building. Then there was the Irish book store, an Indian-owned manufacturing company, a Nigerian insurance agency owner, an African import business, several non-profits, an Indian arts group, an Indian newspaper, a shampoo company, and so on. I had such a good blend of tenants over the years. Many companies grew out of the building and relocated. The project received a lot of positive press. It was great watching people's reactions when I gave tours.

There was no building like this one, anywhere.

In the 1980s there were few financial institutions that had know-how and interest in inner-city development. Most investors, both individual and commercial, favored the growing first-tier and emerging second-tier suburbs. This was where the action was, they believed. That's why leadership for inner-city redevelopment had to come from foundations and government. It was hard to attract new private investment until it was clear that crime was down and neighborhoods had stabilized.

What was overlooked by investors was the buying power and expertise that existed in these neighborhoods. Those potential assets were there, waiting for someone like Brenda to organize and pull them all together. Where such leaders appeared, islands of opportunity surfaced along select commercial corridors such as Franklin Avenue. Brenda's leadership emerged at exactly the time when it was most needed, and could have the greatest impact.

A typical landlord story in an incubator: The city called one day. They had these young college guys that were making cool clothes, baggy jeans, and so on, and they needed 6,000 square feet of space. I happened to have one vacancy. I took a chance and moved them in. They were called "Thump Inc." Their business took off when MTV became a big buyer. They opened another shop on Hennepin Avenue called the Lava Lounge. Later they moved to Hollywood and became millionaires, I hope. They started in my building. Pretty exciting stuff! In total, we built over 108,000 square feet of space. The shopping center was 52,000 square feet, and the business center 56,000.

One big problem arose when Country Club went out of business, and we were left with 30,000 square feet of space. We wound up cutting the space to 20,000 square-foot and 10,000 square-foot sections, and got a smaller grocery store for a tenant in the 20,000 square-foot section. Then Brueggers Bagels, located in Wisconsin, came to us wanting a Minneapolis location. One of the head guys,

Kurt, was also a person who wanted to help disadvantaged neighborhoods. They started in a tiny office behind Chicago and Franklin. We remodeled the space next to the grocery store for their baking operation, and then we designed space in the business center for their head offices. They wound up with their major facilities on Franklin Avenue.

It was 1997, and I had been there twenty-two years. I was getting tired and I didn't want to build any more, so I gave the board of directors my one-year notice. I was doing everything by then. I was the leasing agent, the manager, the fundraiser. I was a good leasing agent in a difficult commercial area. Usually a business center is 60 percent leased by the end of the first year, and I was 80 percent. By the second year, I had people waiting in line. I even wrote a book on incubator management. I had seen Franklin Avenue go up and then down and then back up again, and it was time to leave. I had won all the awards and met all the people. I did a damned good job. I'm proud of what I did. The old hippie made it. She wasn't supposed to, but she did. I still have many good memories.

After retirement from AIBDC, Brenda did consulting and development work for several years. Her legacy remains for all to see on Franklin Avenue. New development has taken place both to the east and west of her shopping center and business incubator near Maria's Café at 1113 East Franklin Avenue. Brenda's contribution is best summarized by the following tribute given when she received the St Thomas Aquinas medallion from the University of St. Thomas in 1992:

> *Brenda St. Germaine, for nearly 20 years you have worked tirelessly and unselfishly to create better lives for American Indians in Minneapolis by providing jobs, services and meaningful opportunities to improve their livelihoods. You have infused a neighborhood with pride, the kind of pride that can be measured visibly by a bustling shopping center that meets the community's needs and by a small business incubator for tenants,*

who in your words, are doing wonderful things.. . . Your efforts reap unanimous and unqualified praise.

"Brenda is the one who gets the big things moving," one tenant told Corporate Report magazine. "Brenda is one of the people who hold up the sky over the corners of the city," added a foundation official. We are fond of a description by a magazine writer who called you "a complicated bunch of willingness, rambunctiousness and compassion who is absolutely driven to spruce up her corner of the planet." Spruce up, indeed! Our community is fortunate to have such a determined entrepreneur who isn't intimidated by big challenges and difficult times.

MIKE TEMALI

C oming home was going into the basement of a church that had a non-profit in it, or going to a community center. The people I meet in places like that are so unpretentious and down-to-earth and full of interesting characteristics, stories and energy. They are all fighters in the same way that I am a fighter. I am going to fight for my one block, or this one family, or for this little business. That's my crowd!

– Mike Temali, May 2005.

My visit with Mike Temali in May 2005 reminded me of the story called "Acres of Diamonds in Your Own Back Yard." Mike wandered the country in search of direction, only to find the out-let for his incredible passion right back home where he started. He is the founder and executive director of the Neighborhood Development Center in St. Paul.

The Neighborhood Development Center identifies potential entrepreneurs who may be operating micro enterprises out of their homes, and who have the work ethic, technical skills, and entrepreneurial ideas to start, manage, and grow a business. The center provides micro-enterprise training along with financial and technical assistance. Nearly 3,200 entrepreneurs have been assisted, and more than 400 new businesses the center has served are thriving today, creating more that $29 million in economic activity in the Twin Cities each year.

There is a twinkle in Mike's eyes as he relates his escapades around the country. However, as he talks about his own evolution as a force for revitalizing an aging urban commercial corridor, his tone is modest and full of gratitude to the people who helped him along the way. He respects his Yugoslav and Danish background, and with a love for neighborhood and the camaraderie it provided, he endows the community with an amazing ability to create small business entrepreneurs and revitalize economically depressed neighborhoods.

He has that quiet, self-assured quality that reflects an appreciation for his heritage, along with a keen sense of how the world works, or at times, doesn't. You would never guess, other than for periodic cell phone interruptions, that Mike may have as many as ten different community development projects brewing at any given time. His demeanor is relaxed, attentive, and garnished with humor.

There is pride in Mike's voice as he describes his father's role in World War II. That's where his story begins.

My folks are immigrants who came to the United States in the 1950s. My dad was a Yugoslav guerrilla fighter in the underground in World War II. He fought against the Germans, and later against the Communists. He went through extreme hardships during the war, like most people. He spent the last year of World War II in a Gestapo prisoner of war camp in Germany, Stalag 7A. The camp was liberated in 1945 by General Patton. Patton came through and shook the hands of all the officers in the camp. My dad was a lieutenant. He had to stay in Germany for five years after the war because he had fought against Tito, and Tito had won. He was a "Chetnik," as the loyalists to the pre-war Yugoslavian government were called, and any "Chetnik" that tried to return was killed at the border. For five years, he remained in a refugee camp with many others from Eastern Europe.

My mom is from Denmark, and she was a social worker. She had come down from Denmark to work in these camps. She had lost a brother in the war, and Copenhagen, where they lived, had been occupied by the Germans. The hardships that they survived—the loss of country for my dad, loss of a brother for my mom—had a great impact on them, and later on me. My dad was only able to see his parents once after the war, for about ten hours in 1968. He wasn't safe back in Yugoslavia even thirty years later.

My dad had been the chief of police in this displaced persons camp. He and my mom were offered a flight to New York if he would stay on for another six months, so they stayed, and wound up flying to the United States in December 1950. I hold deep in my heart this image of my parents coming here with two packing chests, with the name "Joseph Temali" stenciled on them. I can see them arriving in New York, not knowing the language, sitting at Grand Central Station, waiting for the train to Youngstown, Ohio. I still have one of those chests in my basement.

When they arrived, my dad spoke no English. He was an attorney who spoke nine other languages, but no English. He had been trained to be a diplomat. My mother spoke English, but their only common language when they got married was German. They were sponsored by a Yugoslav in Youngstown, Ohio. There, they worked for three years in a Stanley Iron Works factory, making nuts and bolts and washers. My mom tells how my dad, with his great education, would interview for good jobs, but because he couldn't speak English, he wound up with low-level work. This apparently was devastating for him. Some of this history ties in to what I do today. In a very visceral way, I can relate to recent immigrants who may be driving a taxi cab because they cannot speak English for love or money, but may have three master's degrees and a law degree.

My dad eventually got a job running the gym at a settlement house, Market Street Neighborhood House, in a slum of Louisville, Kentucky. We lived on the fourth floor of this settlement house, a big old warehouse, and that is where I was born in 1954. My parents didn't know a soul there, and their English was still not good. Market Street was the dividing line between a poor white neighborhood and a poor black neighborhood, and it was segregated. The gym was on the white side of the street. One of my dad's first decisions was to open the program up to the black kids from the other side. Some of the whites put graffiti on the wall saying my dad was a nigger lover, but he didn't know enough English to comprehend all that. Some folks thought there would be a lynch mob coming. When you come out of the concentration camps, all that utter devastation, you just don't have any prejudices, at least based on race. Dad had put his life on the line many times during the war, and this incident was not one he was going to back away from because of any petty threats. One of the kids that came to the gym from the black part of town was Cassius Clay, the future heavyweight boxing champion later known as Muhammad Ali. He hung out at the gym a lot, they would talk, and he really bonded with my dad.

It's clear that Mike's parents had a profound influence on the values that shaped his life. Hard work, community service, and the respect one should show for all people, regardless of social or economic standing, are but a few of the lessons they passed on to their son. His recall of these lessons is vivid.

When I was three we moved to St. Paul, to a different settlement house. It was the old Neighborhood House. My dad now realized that he was never going to be able to use his law degree. He applied to the University of Minnesota's School of Social Work, and was accepted. One of his big loves was working with kids, and he was good at that. We moved into an apartment on the third floor of the old building down on the West Side river flats.

So I grew up in St. Paul with parents who had lived through experiences quite different from most of my friends' parents, and there is no question in my mind that their experiences shaped my development. You learn that people live differently in other parts of the world, and have different values. You learn that the entire world can get turned upside down in a hurry. Money or status didn't mean anything to my parents. They were classic immigrants, extremely frugal. From them I learned the importance of human interactions, education, and helping other people.

Dad ran the Neighborhood House youth program, as well as Camp Owindego, a summer camp, where all the West Side kids went. Just recently, I gave a training session to the staff of the Northwest Area Foundation, and Diane Corley, who works for the foundation, came up to me during the break. I had mentioned in my talk that Neighborhood House used to be close by. She said, "Your father would have been so proud of you. I adored your father, and can still picture him walking around Neighborhood House greeting everyone with his thick accent. He would have been very proud of what you do, Mike." That really touched me. My dad died about six years ago at age eighty-four, and I was never quite sure he fully understood what I do. My line of work is always a little hard to describe. My mom is still living, and has recently traveled to Denmark and just returned from Costa Rica, so she is still getting around.

After three or four years, we moved to the east side of St. Paul. By then, my dad spoke better English, but he also spoke Italian. There were Mexican immigrant families there, and my dad would go door-to-door and push these families hard to prepare their kids for college. Italian was close enough to Spanish, so they understood him pretty well. Some would say, "My kids can't go to college because we are Mexicans." He would tell them, "Baloney, your kids can go to college!" He set up a scholarship fund named after Constance Curry, who had worked at Neighborhood House. To this day, the Constance Curry Scholarship Fund sends Latino kids to college. One of the families that benefited from this was the Cervantez family. Manuel Cervantez is now the city attorney for the City of St. Paul, and his brother Jose oversees all municipal buildings in the city of Minneapolis. They were two kids who went to Macalester on that scholarship.

Until age six, I lived in settlement houses. Then we moved

just across the river to Dayton's Bluff on the East Side, because the city tore down the West Side river flats. That whole neighborhood was torn down. To this day, that action by the city is resented by the people who lived there. The reason they gave for tearing down the neighborhood was flooding. However, as soon as they moved everyone out, they put up a flood wall. Then it became dry land, and the city put in an industrial park. So essentially, they wiped out an entire low-income Latino, Mexican, and Jewish neighborhood. People always talk about "Rondo" being wiped out, the African American neighborhood that Interstate 94 cut through just west of the Capitol, but people on the West Side went through the same thing.

In Mounds Park by Dayton's Bluff, there was a small version of that when they brought I-94, with its eight lanes, through the East Side of St. Paul. That freeway wiped out many rows of houses, miles long. It took out the entire leadership of the area where I lived. I grew up watching bulldozers take down my neighborhood, and I had a strong reaction to that.

We lived just where the freeway makes its final S curve after leaving downtown St. Paul. My mother was a social worker with the St. Paul public schools, and prior to that, a social worker at Mount Airy housing project behind Regions Hospital. I spent my whole childhood exposed to housing projects, Neighborhood House, Camp Owindego, and the Mounds Park area. The environment where I lived and my parents worked was subsequently called "inner city." Nobody looked at it that way then. At Gustavus Adolphus College as a freshman, the professor asked the class, "Where are you from?" All the students were from this suburb or that suburb. I answered that I was from St. Paul, and he asked, "What suburb?" It was the first time I realized that not everybody lived where I did.

I believe that love of his home and the neighborhood where he grew up had a profound influence on Temali's career. The characters he describes could be out of a novel. They are his heroes.

The East Side was very blue collar and very white. A typical guy may have worked at Hamm's brewery, liked to hunt, and may have had a snowmobile and a small cabin up north. That was the majority population at the recreation centers and at school. By comparison, the Temali family must have looked extremely exotic. My parents still had thick accents and old ways of raising my brother and me. We had to be home early, be very polite to others, and not have our hands in our pockets. It was Old World and old school formality. In my dad's day you wore a suit to school and when the teacher came in, you stood up and greeted him as mister so-and-so. If you missed an assignment, the teacher would take out a stick and whack your hand. That was my dad's experience base.

He was utterly blown away by the late 1960s and early 1970s. I graduated from Harding High School in 1972. It was the hippie era, when teachers wore casual clothes and students went to school in old blue jeans, wore long hair, and protested against the Vietnam War. The contrast between the student scene, the workers in the neighborhood, and my family was really something. That made for a pretty interesting set of forces going to work on me. I definitely took bits and pieces from each of those. Maybe that is why I have never been attracted to extremism. The specter of World War II hanging over our family showed me where extremist movements like Nazism and Communism could lead. While I was a rock-and-roll kind of guy in the 1960s, I was never a movement type of guy. I did attend a few anti-war rallies, but immediately disconnected because I saw some intolerant mob psychology in play. I wasn't for the war, but I didn't see much intelligent thinking or debate in the anti-war movement, either.

Throughout college I was very negative about suburban sprawl. Not only did I not like suburban-type environments, but it also seemed to me that such environments were being built at the expense of neighborhoods like mine. The people I grew up with were either left behind or wiped out. So I did have kind of an activist philosophy, but it was always funneled through and rooted in neighborhood, on-the-ground activity, real people doing what was best for their friends and neighbors. It was never towards big movements. What always felt like coming home to me, regardless of where I was off to, was going into the basement of a church that had a non-profit in it, or going to a community center. That's where I grew up, and that's where I relate the best to people. The people I meet in places like that are so unpretentious and down-to-earth and full of interesting characteristics, stories, and energy. They are all fighters in the same way that I am a fighter, which is that I am going to fight for my one block or this one family or for this little business. That's my crowd!

My dad was president of the board at that church. The whole scene my father came out of was not exactly partisan, but it was very conservative. I picked up many things from both my parents, but one of the biggest is to stay committed to your values and convictions. Anybody who went through that World War II scene like they did really risked everything for their beliefs. Otherwise, why not just switch sides, when the other guy is coming at you with all those guns? You stick together, and you stick with what you believe.

Eventually, my dad was part of a committee that established the St. Paul chapter of "Big Brothers of America." When it was chartered, he was asked to be the executive director. That was his big break. For the first fifteen years of that organization, he remained its executive director. I learned a ton from him about what it takes to run a non-profit, avoiding conflicts of interest, and keeping personal stuff a million miles away from your non-profit. He made it clear that though he was executive director, the organization belonged to a lot of people, and it served low-income people. It was not "my budget" or "my program." While he was responsible for its management, the organization was owned by the community it served. He also advised staying absolutely neutral in politics. I get asked almost daily to back this candidate or that candidate, and I tell them the same thing my dad taught me: I run a non-profit, and don't get committed to candidates. I need to be able to work with everybody. I watched him work his annual banquet and manage his budget. Now I worry about my budget, and face many of the same issues.

My dad was well known among the politicians and civic leaders. On the board of Neighborhood House were F.K. Weyerhaeuser and his wife. They befriended my parents. They loved my mom and dad, and Mrs. Weyerhaeuser remained friends with my mom until her death a few years ago. In 1963, they sent us all to Europe on their nickel because we couldn't afford to go back and see our relatives. I suspect Weyerhaeuser must have connected my dad here and there, because before long, he was appointed by various governors to develop community education. This had been so successful in Europe that the word had spread to this country. My dad became well known. A lot of people really respected my dad and his commitment to kids. He would put a lot of responsibility on them. He was never a bleeding heart or a handout kind of guy. He was very strict, stern, and demanding. In the era of pretty extensive liberalism and social welfare expansion, his strictness and emphasis on personal responsibility was a real breath of fresh air.

From both my dad and my mom came this notion that no one is better than anyone else, and you never treat anyone better than anyone else. The politicians Dad knew were no better in his mind than the janitor at the office or the guy that ran the elevator. That wasn't just his philosophy. It was in his bones. He had fought next to the janitor as well as next to the senator. In the setting he came out of, that didn't matter. What did matter was the courage and honesty of a person. Being raised in that environment, I learned to respect low-income people immensely. They are every bit as smart and capable as the people at the Minneapolis Club.

I was heavily into Boy Scouts. It made a huge impression on me. I was an Eagle Scout. I also worked as a camp counselor for nine summers, through junior high and college. These were camps for inner city kids, involving a lot of wilderness and outdoors stuff. To this day, I do a lot of outdoor things, like camping in Alaska, Colorado, and the boundary waters of Minnesota. My scout master for four years, Les Walter, was a mentor to me. He was this very down-to-earth painter, and a World War II veteran. He was a leader, about five-foot-six, tough as nails, and had a huge family with nine kids. He was strict and firm, but also a lot of fun, as long as you stayed within proper boundaries of behavior. If you crossed those boundaries, watch out! You'd be in a world of hurt! He never put it on you as though you were a bad kid. It was more like, if you cross the line, you will wash dishes for the next three nights for eighty people here. He was a matter-of-fact disciplinarian. We camped out twelve months a year, which wasn't exactly hip in the 1960s when we didn't have $500 sleeping bags. He was a big influence on me.

To this day, I have an inner circle of five male friends. I got married six years ago, and at the wedding I had five best men. Three of the five I have known since seventh grade, a fourth since ninth grade, and the last I met in college.

One of these guys is Jerry Leis. He is the brother of the second one of the five, Marvin. Jerry has been a role model for me. He is about fourteen years older than me. There were seven kids in that family. Their dad was a janitor, and their mom an aide at a nursing home. Those nine people lived in a small house on the East Side close to my house. They were very poor, but good as gold. Marvin as a kid was my long-term very best friend. From him, I learned a lot about friendship, commitment, tolerance, and working through any problems that might come up in a family. To this day, because of that example, I am more tolerant of some of the small business entrepreneurs we train when they miss a deadline or another problem comes up. I try very hard to see the whole person.

Marvin's older brother Jerry would tone me down on some of my teenage ramblings and philosophizing about how bad television was, or whatever had my ire up. He would turn to me and say, "Mike, have you heard of the off button?" He had a way of reminding me of my own personal responsibility and the choices I could make in life. My last two years of college were at Macalester. In those times, with a liberal education, it was easy to demonize mainstream society as being uncaring and materialistic. Jerry Leis was very influential in taking some of the edge and bitterness over all of that out of me.

The evolution of Mike Temali's political philosophy is refreshing. He wound up rejecting many of the long-winded convictions on both the left and right, in favor of a pragmatic stance. In short, he became a "take care of your home town first" kind of guy. Though he does have political preferences, his time and energy are focused on those things that are within his power to change. Mike actually lives his politics. Though he is remarkably sensitive to human needs, he also possesses the hard-headedness and skill needed to repair his community and move people to self-sufficiency.

Another thing that influenced me when I was a freshman at Gustavus was the Nixon/McGovern election. Most of the students believed, as I did, that McGovern was a saint and Nixon was a crook. It was pretty disillusioning when it turned out that McGovern only won two states. I had to wake up and accept the fact that not everyone felt the same way as I did about many issues, but they were still good people. This is what has been pushing me throughout my career—to work on the street level, one business at a time, and not fret about which way the world is going. When George W. Bush won his first and second election, I didn't vote for him, but it didn't ruin my life. It is sort of irrelevant, if you are working with real people on the ground.

I haven't really changed my basic moderate-to-liberal beliefs. The late Sen. Paul Wellstone was about the only politician I ever really engaged with at a personal level. He was so genuine and sincere. I could certainly make him a hero or role model, not so much for his agenda or stand on the issues, but for the way he engaged people with so much love, passion, compassion, and enthusiasm. That to me is what public service is all about. He was motivated to do his thing, the way I am motivated to do my thing. It isn't ultimately about big-picture politics, or liberal this or conservative that. It is about, "Can't we all agree that Joe Six Pack or Juan the immigrant from Mexico or Mohammed from Somalia ought to be able to get a good job, and ought to be able to start a new business, and yes, needs to learn English, and needs to pay taxes?" That is the kind of thing that liberals and conservatives can agree on. If my career had gone in a more political direction, I think I would have spent my life being depressed! The country has gone in a more conservative direction and become a lot more mean-spirited and short-sighted, but that doesn't need to cripple me, because of the choice I made early on. I am not going to spend my life mad or depressed, and I don't hang around people that do!

My feelings while at Gustavus were mixed. Early on, it reinforced my dislike of suburbs. Most of the students there were into partying, which I wasn't very good at. I did my share, but I wasn't into the social scene. I have never been a group person, and was about as far from ever wanting to join a fraternity as anyone could imagine. Gustavus was a big fraternity and sorority place. I found one or two close friends, and we all wound up leaving the same year.

I really enjoyed my two years at Macalester. My major was sociology with two core concentrations, one in philosophy and one in political science. That was when John B. Davis was president. The first day I arrived on campus, the African American students had occupied the administration building, so it was pretty exciting. When Saigon fell at the end of the Vietnam War, someone put a banner outside my dorm proclaiming victory. I had a very negative reaction to that. While I was against the war, I wasn't about to feel happy that communists had taken over South Vietnam. That just appalled me. That little snapshot gives you a good sense of where I did and didn't fit into the late 1960s and early 1970s. My dad had fought Communists, and our church was filled with refugees from communism, and many of our priests had been routinely killed by communists in Yugoslavia. We looked at these college kids as being naïve at best, and traitors at worst.

After college, I roamed the country with four other guys. I hitchhiked all over the West for three months, from St. Paul to Montana, with my skis on my shoulder. That's the same way I visited Mexico, with twenty dollars in my pocket. My folks thought I was doing these trips with a friend in a car.

For a couple of years, I did a lot of odd jobs. I drove a school bus for one year, and was a carpenter for six months. I hitchhiked to Seattle, and then down to San Diego. I thought I was going to go to work for Cesar Chavez and the farm workers. One night, I was sleeping by a river outside of Yakima, Washington, with a hobo named Blue, and he sat up all night telling me about his life. I spent a lot of time with the real down-and-out drifters. When you have experiences like this, you wind up later in life just looking at people differently. Today, I look out my office window on University and Dale and see distressed people, and say, "There but for the love of God go me." After all, how far are any of us from needing a helping hand?

Those experiences in my formative years, rubbing shoulders with the kind of folks that maybe now are coming into my program, made me a more effective social entrepreneur. My style has always been to be very practical and experimental, not reluctant to try new approaches, after evaluating the risks involved. Today, I am trying to put $16 million together to do the Global Market at the old Sears site on Lake Street, and I feel pretty sanguine about it. I explain the challenges to the various investors, but I know that my job is not to guarantee success, but to lay out as clearly as possible the risks and rewards of the project. If it fails, I will be very disappointed and lose some sleep, but it won't permanently interfere with my life's work. I'm sort of the antithesis of your normal salesman. Many of these inner-city deals are tough to do, but when one of them works, it's really cool! I've lost money personally in lousy business deals, so I have a good sense of entrepreneurial risk.

Near the end of my wandering days, my mother clipped out an article about VISTA and said, "Mike, why don't you try this?" So I signed up to be a VISTA volunteer, and ended up spending a year in San Bernardino, California. That was a very important experience for me, since I was not used to working indoors, or having break- fast with an office worker instead of a truck driver. I was in a legal services office, and for the first week or two I was terribly uncomfortable. They parked me next to attorneys that were doing things that I found interesting. There were a couple of major efforts that I wound up leading. One was a rent control movement in San Bernardino, which came on the heels of Proposition 13. Howard Jarvis had promised rent rollbacks across California if Proposition 13 passed. The day after it passed, rents doubled and tripled all across California. I was involved in all the dialogue and organizing that followed. Another major event was the passage of the Community Reinvestment Act by the Congress in 1977. My job was to assemble data on home ownership and mortgage availability in low-income neighborhoods. We eventually brought together a number of ethnic groups and filed one of the first actions in the country against California Savings and Loan. They were very responsive, and built a branch bank in the Chicano/Black half of San Bernardino, which at that time was not served by any bank. All the loans from San Bernardino banks were going up to the mountain resort area of Arrowhead and Big Bear. It was a very tangible result of the year's work, seeing a new bank in that part of town with loan officers and a bilingual manager. I was pictured in the newspaper as "The Citizen in the Sun" for one week. I still have the headline framed which read, "$260 a Month for Picking These Fights."

With the encouragement of friends and the support of my parents, I applied at the Humphrey Institute and received a Humphrey Fellowship. From 1979 to 1981 I studied there, and also interned at the Urban Coalition with the late Earl Craig and Peter McLaughlin, now Hennepin County commissioner. Steve Cramer, a future Minneapolis City Council member, was another Humphrey student interning with me at the Urban Coalition. Others there included Luanne Nyberg, John Pacheco, Vusi Zulu, and Ron McKinley. It was quite a crowd. I was the little new guy on the scene.

I had a series of community internships throughout college and graduate school. At the Humphrey, one of my four classes every semester would be an internship out in the community. I obtained a federal grant to put solar panels on two non-profits, The City Inc.

and Turning Point, and I trained people in Red Wing in the use of solar energy. Another internship involved the Energy Mobilization Office in St. Paul with Alice Murphy, when George Latimer was mayor. Much earlier, while at Macalester, I had done an internship with the Cedar Riverside Environmental Defense Fund with Jack Cann and Charlie Warner, when Heller-Segal was trying to put up all those tall buildings in Cedar Riverside.

Mike enjoyed his mix of service work and study in graduate school, and began to consider an academic career. But the negative reception that greeted a study done by his advisor, Cal Bradford, of the public-private partnership called City Venture, Inc., spearheaded by Control Data, changed Mike's mind.

By this time, 1984, I was approaching thirty. I needed to figure out what I was going to do with the rest of my life. I wrote down on the back of an envelope all the things I liked. Community involvement and economic development work rose to the top of the list. An architect friend of mine, Al Raymond, was working with Ruth Murphy at the Community Design Center. He told me that they were forming a new organization in St. Paul trying to revitalize Rice Street, and said that I should apply for the job. The idea didn't turn me on. I was an East Side kid, and knew little about Rice Street. We were not all that familiar with the other neighborhoods. Al Raymond put me in his car and drove me around back roads off Rice Street. It blew my mind that these little twenty-foot-wide lots, with houses that were almost leaning against each other off Sycamore and Atwater Streets, were backed up against railroad tracks, junk yards, and some heavy industrial facilities. Rice Street itself was almost boarded up at the time. I had always thought that the tough work I wanted to do would be in the South Bronx or on one of the Native American reservations, where folks were poor. That little tour Al gave me that day convinced me that I didn't have to look far to find real poverty, or a worthwhile and challenging opportunity. I applied for the job. At the time, I was on the board of the Powderhorn Residents Group in south Minneapolis, where I was living. There was a woman on the board who was also applying for the job. She wound up getting accepted. Then she called me and said something to the effect that she didn't believe in capitalism, and wasn't going to take the job. She bowed out, I was offered the job, and that's how all of this got started. That trip down Rice Street was the single greatest break of my life.

From the first day I started there—June 1, 1984—I felt like I was back home. I just adored the job. My starting salary was $30,000. Al Raymond and Ruth Murphy had gotten a grant from the St. Paul Companies for exactly $30,000. Dennis Prchal, who was exactly my age, was the president of the board. Denny was a banker with Western Bank and president of the board of the North End Businessmen's Club. This was truly an "old boys" board, with guys puffing on their cigars and complaining about welfare. Most of these men were in their fifties and sixties. Some were somewhat embittered about social changes that had left them off to the side. They were depressed that Rice Street wasn't successful anymore. At the same time, while some were current with new business practices, others were not keeping up with marketing trends or newer approaches to customer service. Nevertheless, I loved these guys to death, because they were the type of folks I had grown up with. We were able to relate to one another. I was able to convince them to put up a new sign in front of their building while we chatted about the Twins or Vikings. My academic experience was a godsend, but I kept all that below the surface and focused on building solid relationships. Denny Prchal continued to be my boss, and to this day is one of my closest friends and mentors. He still runs Western Bank's Insurance Agency, and is president of Sparc, [formerly NEAR, North End Area Revitalization] the name we gave our program.

For six years, I ran a one-person office right in the heart of Rice Street, and was responsible for a one-mile stretch of Rice Street from the railroad tracks north of University all the way north to Maryland. At the time there were about a hundred commercial structures on the corridor, forty of which were boarded up. What I figured out early was that every building had a story, as did every person. Their stories were just as complicated and involved as anything I had been working on at the Humphrey Institute. Every one of these business owners had ambitions, plans and attitudes, as well as friends and enemies.

I wound up trying to buy three buildings from a guy who was running a prostitution ring out of his restaurant. He was very smart and rugged. Given my background as a carpenter and hitchhiker, I was pretty well armed to deal with these guys. I felt right at home with the roughest and weirdest of the crowd, and had all the guidance I needed from Denny Prchal and the board. This was a great board that included Gene Fashiona, a printer named Dan Jeans, Tom Hupert, and others who were not only successful in business, but were imbedded in the power structure of Rice Street.

There was one business owner who tested me by telling me how things worked at his end of Rice Street. He called me in and basically told me that he called the shots at this end of town, and I would take orders from him. I had to look him in the eye and let him know that that wasn't how things would work, that I reported to a board that met once a month, and they were in charge. I told him that if he had issues, I would take them to the board and he would get a fair hearing. In time, he became one of my staunchest allies.

Rice Street had lost a couple of hardware stores, a furniture store, two drug stores, and was in the process of emptying out. Downtown Rice Street was dying. One of the survivors was the Munteen Department Store. It was into the second generation, run by three Munteen brothers who had taken over from their father. Their business was tapering off. They had no debt on the building, but they were not reinvesting in the business. The place looked like a scene out of the 1930s. Paul Munteen was the treasurer of NEAR, and when I would go to pick up my check every two weeks, he would read me the riot act about how nothing was happening. He may have been joking. He was Rumanian Orthodox and there was this little Rumanian church he used to take me to, just off Rice Street. He brought me to their banquet once and introduced me as this fine young Serbian Orthodox boy. One day I heard sirens and followed them to the store, and Paul was lying dead on the floor. There was so much of that. I felt so close to these people, all trying to make it on this one little street.

What we did worked very well. Our first effort was to hit it hard with about a dozen storefront façade projects in the summer of 1984. The strategy was to get a lot of small projects done quickly, a sign here, a new storefront there, and a paved parking lot across the street. We needed to show visible progress. With every one of these people, it was a negotiation. Ruth Murphy and Al Raymond also raised $180,000 from the city of St. Paul for neighborhood development. Of this, $120,000 was available for loans at 2 percent interest, and the balance for grants. For every deal, we would do a 50 percent grant up to $2,000, and a loan at 2 percent interest for 75 percent of the balance. The owner would put up the rest. Over my six years there, we did 80 of these deals with only one default. Our business model was to stay lean, help with the plan or idea, lend and make grants, and then expedite with technical assistance. We were very flexible about design, so long as things wound up looking better. The entire philosophy was to create a lot of rapid visible change that would alter people's perception, and stimulate and leverage much larger change later. A lot of what I do today is based on that philosophy of creating visible change.

When you are in community development, you are a drop in the bucket at best. Even in a population of ten thousand low-income people, you might have a $66 million economy. That results from 3,300 households having an average household income of $20,000. With a war chest of $180,000 and one guy's time, you have to generate many small visible examples of positive change to have any impact at all. It has to look private, and not like some big governmental development. You are trying to jumpstart people's mindset, and help them realize that after all these years, something really is happening. That's when businesses begin to believe it can happen, and start investing in their future.

After two years, we came up with another loan program that financed business expansion. We surveyed each business, and asked them to lay out their plans for the future. There were a host of issues related to personalities and space that had to be resolved to help these businesses expand. The same formula applied on the financing, as well as the notions that other neighborhoods were doing this, and if you work with Temali, you can get fast action and avoid dealing with the bureaucracy. We did have some businesses move out, and I would spend hours on the phone cold calling new prospects and letting them know about the kind of support they would have if they moved to Rice Street. I would solicit bicycle shops, hardware stores, furniture dealers, drug stores and others, telling about the full-service approach we were bringing to the area. Out of about two thousand phone calls I made, we landed ten new businesses.

The next program we had was a streetscape project. We raised $250,000 for benches, banners and lighting, and so forth. Finally, we took on the big one, which was trying to create more retail space at the corner of Rice and Front streets. Three houses and two dilapidated commercial buildings were torn down, and we built the North End Center, a small-scale retail center. We then added a pharmacy, a Subway sandwich shop, a liquor store, and a family restaurant, and attached it all to an existing Super America. By the time I left six years later, there had been a visible transformation of Rice Street. Almost every building had a new façade, there were new businesses, nearly all the boards were off those older buildings, and there were marketing campaigns going on up and down the street. There was a lot of new energy on Rice Street.

I was approached by Bill Sands, chairman & CEO of Western Bank, that same year, to put together a community development operation at his bank. He was committed to being a community banker, and wanted to see the surrounding neighborhoods do better. Joe Errigo, who ran Common Bond, was on his board, as was my friend Denny Prchal. They recruited me to start this development corporation and told me that I would have $100,000 to start with, and when that was gone, I would also be gone. Bill Sands and I went to Chicago and visited the South Shore Bank, which was well known for being successful in revitalizing poor neighborhoods. What we decided to focus on was capacity building with a number of community-based organizations around the Twin Cities. Our strategy was to use the NEAR model, because of the success on Rice Street. What NEAR brought to light was the notion that business revitalization was key to successful long-term economic development. Prior to that time, the emphasis had been more on housing and family assistance. There were a number of other business clubs from other commercial corridors that wanted to learn about NEAR'S success. That is how WIND, Western Initiatives for Neighborhood Development, got started. It was only the second development corporation in the state operating under a bank charter.

For two years, I followed that model. I helped the Selby Area Community Development Corporation (CDC), get started with staffing, fund raising, getting a loan fund for façade grants, and training their board. A lot of our work was on the West Side of St. Paul, transforming the Concord Street Business Association into what is now known as The Riverside Economic Development Association. The branding of Concord Street as "District del Sol" came from that organization, and I spent about ten hours a week working with them.

By 1992 I was tired of consulting and looking for more hands-on involvement. I heard about a study that Greg Finzell and the District Eight Planning Council had done with the University of Minnesota called the SNAP Survey, Summit-University Needs Assessment Project. One of the questions they asked residents was if they ran a business out of their home. Eleven percent said yes, which meant that about 1,100 of the 10,000 people in the Selby-Dale neighborhood were entrepreneurial. At about the same time, Bill Sands sent me on a trip to Indonesia and Thailand with then-Gov. Rudy Perpich's economic trade mission. With the help of

Nancy Latimer at the McKnight Foundation, I was able to study micro-enterprise organizations as we traveled. I brought back some techniques for training and financing small entrepreneurs.

The next year was spent developing this concept for our own neighborhoods, working with the board of WIND—people like Beverly Hawkins, Dave Gagne, Denny Prchal, Bill Sands, Brenda St. Germaine, Patti Totozintle and Joe Errigo. Our approach—a mix of micro-enterprise development and neighborhood development—was unique at that time in the United States. Our goal was to work with home-based entrepreneurs in a way that helped them become more viable and remain in their neighborhood, creating clusters. We set it up so that they could develop contacts with the Selby Area CDC, which I was working with at the time. These entrepreneurs had trust in their local CDC. The same concept was applied to NEAR and the West Side. We started training people in the offices of their own neighborhood associations or CDC, and then the associations would help them get their businesses launched.

Fairly soon thereafter, we tried to start our own loan program for these graduates, because they were not bankable at the time. Our timing was fortuitous. At that same time, 1994, Governor Arne Carlson was reacting to the Rodney King riots in Los Angeles by creating an Urban Initiative Loan Program for Minnesota. We were one of the first organizations to partner with the state of Minnesota on urban initiative loans. The McKnight Foundation followed up with a $600,000 matching grant. So we had $1.2 million in loan money to assist entrepreneurs coming out of our own classes. Once that was in place, we realized that many of these entrepreneurs needed management and technical assistance for months after their businesses got started. That is how the three program legs of the Neighborhood Development Center got started—outreach through neighborhood partners, training and financing, and finally, one-on-one technical assistance after the business is launched.

By 1996, we realized that we needed to start doing this in other languages. We started in Spanish on the West Side, with all women, and then in south Minneapolis at Saint Stephen's Church. The class at St. Stephen's was organized by Catholic Charities' organizers Sal Miranda and Juan Linares. We also hooked up with John Flory of the Whittier Neighborhood CDC, who was experienced in community economic development. Because the attendees were in a place they trusted, Sal and Juan were able to survey their strengths and assets, and counsel them about what type of business might work for them in an economy dominated by different cultural norms.

Several of the graduates of our sixteen-week entrepreneurial business plan classes at St. Stephen's that were presented in Spanish got together and said, "We want to do a mercado." We had no idea of what a mercado was at the time. The Mercado Central at Lake Street and Bloomington opened in 1999. It was the dream of those graduate entrepreneurs, and they were the ones that started businesses there. It has been six years now, and they have had an 80 percent success rate. More than 40 percent of them have started second locations. They generate in excess of $6 million of sales annually. They are not big, and operate in small spaces, but for most of them it is the first rung up the ladder. Now we just completed Plaza Verde, the old Antiques Minnesota building across the street from the Mercado Central on Lake Street in Minneapolis. Several of the Mercado folks have stepped up the ladder into 1,000-2,000–square-foot space in Plaza Verde. Their market has broadened as well. Now, after having developed the tools for this first stage of outreach, training and technical assistance, we are working on helping these entrepreneurs grow their businesses.

The final phase will be to get their financial situation to a point where they are bankable. We have La Torterilla Le Perla, founded by Jose Payan, who started washing dishes and cooking, and who opened a shop at the Mercado with one tortilla machine. He has opened a second shop on Payne Avenue, and now he is buying a million dollar building in south Minneapolis and adding $800,000 of equipment. This is an entrepreneur who will have fifty employees. There is another man who started out washing dishes at the Minneapolis Club and started a business at the Mercado, and is now grossing $1 million a year at his little restaurant, La Hacienda. We feel good about participating in this explosion of immigrant businesses on Lake Street, Payne Avenue, and University Avenues.

Our current project, The Midtown Global Market, at the old Sears site in south Minneapolis, will have sixty-two businesses of every ethnicity, with all types of ethnic foods—kind of like Pike's Place Market in Seattle or Reading Terminal Market in Philadelphia. It will have space for start-up businesses, for people coming through our training class, and expansion space for businesses that outgrow the Mercado. The key is to have these entrepreneurs continue to grow their marketing, accounting, production and management skills, so that they can continue to be successful.

The final aspect of our business to become significant is real estate, where we house our business incubators, and provide technical assistance. University and Dale will continue to have our attention because we live there. We convened the five-neighborhoods collaborative that is developing the old Faust site on the southwest corner of University and Dale. We are also developing the five-story project on the northeast corner of University and Dale that will have commercial enterprises on the first floor.

When we first started the Neighborhood Development Center, I was the only employee. Now we have eighteen employees with five full-time lenders. All along the way Bill Sands has been a mentor and advisor to me. He provided the platform for all I have worked on since 1990. I still enjoy community building and seeing people improve themselves. Now I have two small children and have been married for six years. Some of these sixty-hour weeks are a little bit over the edge. At age 51, I feel very fortunate to have had these opportunities, and expect to stay at it for many years to come. My book on community development is in its second printing. They are turning it into a textbook, now, with test questions for college and graduate school students. This morning I presented the Global Marketplace story to ten of the largest businesses in Minnesota. That is our biggest project yet. So the momentum continues.

ATUM AZZAHIR

The context for my story is my people, my culture, and my heritage. My life story is about the hands and unbreakable spirit of my parents, Eldrid and Canniebell Shack, who are responsible for the shaping of who I have become. I can only speak to what I do with what they have given me.

– Atum Azzahir, March 2007

As someone three generations removed from the enslavement of her people, Atum Azzahir has lived long enough to know that the perils and joys of life are incredible gifts, full of meaning and purpose—gifts, according to Azzahir, which contain useful knowledge and insight. Her life's journey has taken her from the harsh realities of the Jim Crow South, where the spirits of her father and other black men were under relentless and malicious attack; to the intense resistance of the civil rights struggle of the 1960s; to the feminist movement of the 1980s; and finally, to a deeply spiritual process of cultural recovery, a process which Azzahir says occurs when people of African heritage reconnect to the culture that was lost to them during 400-plus years spent in bondage.

Azzahir's life and work as a community organizer have given her profound understanding of how a beleaguered human spirit can be transformed. Her understanding is based on personal experience: Azzahir watched her father spat upon and demeaned throughout his entire life, and yet retain a peaceful, gentle, and kind personality that became her inspiration.

Her journey through personal loss and tragedy has not been in vain. It has given her penetrating insight into how to break the hold that anger and victimization have on her people, and to develop the skills needed to build a better life. As a pioneer in the process of creating health, wealth, and community cohesion through cultural transformation, Azzahir says that culture is the apparatus for launching people from the depths of dependency to the heights of self-respect and self-reliance. Azzahir wants to establish her organization as the leading authority on cultural approaches to personal and community health. When decision makers learn that helping communities build their own cultural knowledge yields positive, lasting change, says Azzahir, the payoff to our economy and quality of life will be enormous.

We met at Atum's office at the Powderhorn Phillips Cultural Wellness Center, on East Lake Street in south Minneapolis, in March 2007. The Center opened to the public in October 1996 as a result of Atum's grassroots organizing, funded by the Medica Foundation. A belief that sickness and disease are the direct result of the absence of community and culture is at the heart of the center's work. Unlike other programs that aim to increase access to health care in the black community, the Cultural Wellness Center attempts to overcome chronic ills by producing personalities that are culturally self-aware, and anchored in the purpose of restoring and maintaining health and wholeness. Atum Azzahir told me the story of her own attainment of such a personality, and her passion for instilling it in others. This is her autobiography.

I was born and raised in Grenada, Mississippi, a small town about a hundred miles south of Memphis, Tennessee. Although we didn't have a life free from misery and struggle, it didn't seem so horrible at the time. I guess you could say things were just the way they were.

My mother, Canniebell, and father, Eldrid, left school at a very early age. My mother did not read or write and my father picked up most of his limited writing and verbal skills while serving in the Army. My father was a very tall man with a joyful disposition, who'd walk around with his hand on my head while telling me stories. Later, with mature intuition, I realized that he did that to deal with the brutality of racism. He was intentionally protecting his spirit by telling stories and using laughter. He was also protecting my spirit by placing the palm of his hand on my head. Now that I have studied my culture, I know that he was transmitting things to me and receiving some, too.

My mother's personality was quite different. She was a domestic worker. She was not going to take bad treatment from anybody. Therefore, finding work was difficult for her. My mother gained a reputation for being "mouthy." As far back as I can remember, she carried a pistol, and people referred to her as a "pistol-packing woman." My father worried that her ferocious attitude would get us into trouble, but actually, white people stayed away from her because they thought she was dangerous, or at least crazy.

When I think about those who influenced me, I have to start with my father. His unwavering determination to protect the spirit and to work from the inside out, despite the racism he encountered, taught me so much. He was a genuine man and a man of God who would not let himself be destroyed by other men. He was born in 1918, and his parents died at an early age. He was raised by relatives. He seemed to inherit a genuine, kind, and deeply spiritual personality. It was just there. We all experience challenges in life, and encounter people who treat us poorly and attempt to break our spirit. It is how we respond to those encounters that makes all the difference. It was probably in my thirties when I finally figured all that out. It took a while for me to recognize that being a victim was not what my dad was all about.

He told us about his return from World War II in 1945, and how he expected to be treated well, like he'd been promised. I saw how he dealt with discovering that the promise was empty, especially after he was denied the benefits accorded to veterans by the GI Bill. He was called bad names, spat on in my presence by men who hired him to do the least desirable jobs, like lawn mowing and trash hauling. He could have justifiably turned out to be a hate-filled and angry person. But he had a personality that could endure, because he could find things to be happy about and grateful for. This is a personality that has its lineage in black heritage, black ancestral ways of being and knowing—in essence, African culture.

Seeing my father mistreated didn't defeat my spirit. It made me a young revolutionary. I did not want to see any black man treated this way. My brother, who is five years older than me, felt the same, but his personality was at this time much more like my mother's. He was outspoken, and would push things to the limit. I learned a lot about how to develop my personality as I watched my brother. I took note of the disgraceful consequences that his upfront attitude would bring him as he tried to directly confront the established white leadership. I learned by watching my brother that our people would never be able to change our circumstances if we allowed ourselves to be constantly reacting to injustice. We had to know how to be active, not reactive. Perhaps this is why I chose to model my attitude and personality more after my father's. This is not to say, however, that I did not have lessons to learn about being too nice and passive. I had to learn how to keep from becoming a doormat to other people's agendas and motivations.

My brother and I went to a segregated school in a totally segregated environment. Everything around us was segregated, including grocery stores, churches, businesses and medical clinics. I remember having to sit in the very rear of the movie theater when we wanted to see a film. I had very little comfortable interaction with white people until I was in my late teens. Segregation was institutionalized throughout the country, but it was especially direct and in-your-face in the South. In Mississippi, we knew that if a white person came into our neighborhood, it was either the police or life insurance salesmen. These salesmen were rip-off artists because nobody ever seemed to collect life insurance when someone died. In my mother's case, she put her money into paying off the mortgage on our house, so at least we had that when she died.

It was due to my father that I did not become angry and lose control during the civil rights movement, even though I was in the center of that movement.

I became pregnant in 1959, at age 16. That is when I left high school. Instead of running off, I stayed home, took care of my baby, and studied, while at the same time doing domestic work for our neighbors. My mother would not let me get married because she felt that it would not be a good match. She also would not let me work in white women's homes because she felt it would break my spirit.

When my first son was born, his father followed the track that he knew: he graduated from high school in 1959, then joined the Army. When he came back on furlough about a year later, I married my child's father. My mother permitted it then because he was in the Army, and had an income and some possibility for us to have a life. Her biggest issue had been that if he couldn't take care of himself, how could he possibly take care of me and the baby? By this time I was 17, and we gave birth to another son. My brother had moved to Milwaukee, and when my husband got out of the Army, he suggested we follow him there. By then Grenada, Mississippi, was becoming dangerous. The civil rights movement was bringing people into the streets, and awakening an ugly response in the white community. My brother demanded that we come north.

By 1963, jobs were starting to open up in Milwaukee, and there was a sense of opportunity and hope for African Americans. We moved there just in time for the civil rights movement to gain real momentum. These were ripe times for activist young people.

There were riots and civil unrest. My own activism took the form of encouraging and inspiring people to create a vision for themselves, and to plan for pursuing their vision, with or without anyone else's permission. I was active in PTA, and helped the nursing assistants I worked with to realize that we could make some positive changes in our status from the inside out. The important thing was to help people realize that to bring about effective change, we had to start with ourselves. My mother's influence reminded me that you don't have to be passive and let people mistreat you. On the other hand, my father's lesson was that you must limit the impact of the things you cannot change from the outside. You can't change, working from the outside; you have to go in. So "keep yourself from being a victim" was my mother, and "If you can't control being victimized, then you must figure out for yourself how to avoid being overcome by it" was my father.

These principles have sustained me as I've organized at schools, the workplace, and in the broader community. In the 1960s, it was the African American community that was being most hurt by the riots and destruction of homes and local businesses. I kept asking the question publicly, "Who are we really hurting?" and "Who are the real victims?" My goal was to get people together to think about this, and not be in the position of begging for freedom. Although by 1964 I was still only twenty-one years old, and had three sons and a husband, yet I had already learned some lasting values as a result of my organizing efforts. When you fight to try to change the system without changing yourself, it becomes overwhelming, and over time, you burn out. When you give yourself freedom and change from the inside out, you have far more strength, greater success, and less intimidation and fear. This is my primary philosophy for how we as a people can get back on our feet.

Having three children at an early age gave me something to strive for. It was the reason I had to work harder and be more responsible. It became the reason I had to make different decisions. I was a part of a group in the neighborhood who worked hard to run their own small businesses. We earned money babysitting and washing dishes for other African American women who had jobs outside the neighborhood. My earnings helped us buy diapers and other household necessities. There was no welfare system in our community, and if there was, we wouldn't have accepted it. We had this fighting spirit to share and make it on our own.

Education had always been an important value in our family. I learned to read and write at an early age, so I was able to help my parents with the normal flow of paperwork and correspondence. My parents must have appreciated this, as they encouraged me to finish my education. There was a white woman whom my mother worked for, over many years. The woman lived well, and through the handling of this woman's affairs, my mother was exposed to some of the finer things in life. She even helped my father get a job. Many times, my mother would tell us at the dinner table that if "they can do what they do, and if they can have what they have, we can also ... They are no smarter than we are." Again, my mother would say, "If I didn't do all the work, she wouldn't have anything. We can do better than they can. We must do better than what they expect." This insight was at the core of my drive to get an education.

Therefore, one of the first things I did when I arrived in Milwaukee was to go back to school and get my GED. As the civil rights movement gained momentum, I struggled to figure out what I could do that would benefit my children in the long-term, and ensure that our dignity was upheld. While people were fighting the school system, my approach was to figure out how we could educate ourselves to create our own jobs. Fighting to change the white power structure and the deeply imbedded white sense of superiority seemed counterintuitive to me. I couldn't imagine people volunteering to give up power, control, and a first-class ride through life. My approach was to work first on myself, going from the inside out.

It was the brutal murder of Emmett Till in 1955 that first made me aware of how dangerous being black could be for me and my family. That event and others like it brought the black community together, and made us aware of how we presented ourselves and watched out for one another. Because of Emmett Till, I spent many years making my children aware of how society worked and how embedded hatred was in white-dominated social structures. I taught them what kinds of situations to avoid. I would say, "This is how some white people are, but how we conduct ourselves.... is what really matters." My greatest concern to this day is that we in the African American community are not protecting ourselves and preventing the violence and killing that still goes on. We have turned the hate onto ourselves. What others have done to us, we now do to each other.

One aspect of Martin Luther King's movement that I loved was the idea of a beloved community. When Dr. King was leading the civil rights movement, he also embraced his family and made sure that their mutual support system remained intact. Leaders had to get out in front and challenge the status quo, but the family also had to be cared for and embraced. That was the part of the movement that gave the whole thing validity for me—the notion that the external fight would not have lasting impact if the internal, spiritual, family-based values were not in place. The people doing the teaching of culture and traditions, such as the churches and other social networks, all had to be part of the effort if real progress was to be made. I watched Dr. King and the civil rights movement from that vantage point. It struck me that in many ways Martin Luther King's philosophy of non-violence mirrored my father's values.

I concluded that the key thing was to have the African American community investing in the internal core of who we are, and what we are; from this building of the core, we could endure and build for the future. It was important for us never to forget that not only are we somebody, we also have something of value. Our value is what is at the core of our fight.

Vietnam for me was a matter of asking oneself, "What are we doing over there, when we have all this confusion back here? You've got a lot of nerve messing around in other people's lives, challenging other nations and imposing political values on others, when so many people are disadvantaged here at home." All of this injustice going on in our neighborhoods, with white people depriving black people, the fighting and the poverty and the riots. What right do we have to tell anybody else how to live, until we clean up our own act?! I felt that way about Vietnam, and I feel the same way today!

We lived in Milwaukee until 1978. I raised four sons and lived through all of the problems of the late 1960s. My work was in health care, and that brought me into contact with a man named John Conway, who ran a home health agency. I did so well that I wound up running that business, placing physicians and nurses in different locations. When my husband got out of the Army, he experienced much of the same rejection by the white population that my father had experienced. With his veteran's benefits, we were able to buy a home in 1968. However, my husband was embittered by the way he was treated after serving his country and, possessing my mother's fiery nature, he had great difficulty fitting in. His frustration and deep personal conflict brought a lot of violence into our home.

It became a very sad period for my family, and I experienced injuries from him. In 1978, I decided that was it. We had been married since 1961, and my oldest son was eighteen and had graduated from Marquette High School. He was very smart and had a scholarship to go to the University of Minnesota. Though it was a difficult decision, I felt it was important to leave this intensely harmful relationship and create a more peaceful life for my children. So I came to Minneapolis on the run. My youngest son was eight, and the oldest was at the university. I was able to find a job as a nursing assistant, and later as a scheduling coordinator, at Deaconess Hospital.

In December 1978, I went back to Milwaukee to visit my brother. My husband found out about it and came over. He was in a rage. He shot me three times, then committed suicide. I was hospitalized, and given little hope for recovery. It was just a horrible experience. I did recover, and we came back to Minneapolis three weeks later.

There was no room inside me for anger. But the question remained, "How do you think about something like this? What would drive someone to do something like this to a loved one, or to himself? What causes that kind of internal struggle?" That's what I wanted to understand. And I decided that it has to do with internalizing how you are viewed from the outside. The way so many black men are treated creates an internal rage over time. I kept asking myself how we could turn this around.

I was given the gift of life for myself and for my children. I also have the gift of meaningful work, which others in my family did not have. I think about my aunts and uncles and grandparents, and the teachings they passed along, and the resiliency they had despite brutal racial oppression, and I feel so blessed to have these things as my great cultural heritage. My father's large hand upon my head provided protection for my mind and safeguarded my spirit from life's brutality. Even through physical and emotional pain, my spirit was protected. I think that can be taught. That is what my life is all about today.

My work at Deaconess Hospital was very rewarding. Friends at my church led me to Minneapolis Technical Institute to work with Charles Nichols, the director of vocational education. I called him and asked him to go out to lunch with me. He still laughs about the fact that this woman who had next to nothing asked him out to lunch, and paid for his lunch. He hired me as a vocational advisor for the Minneapolis Technical Institute. I stayed there for five years, serving people who wanted to be educated but didn't want to go the traditional academic route. The work involved the basics of reading, writing, and developing communication skills, together with knowing what is expected when one ultimately shows up for work. This was a terrific experience.

At the time I was also volunteering with the battered women's movement as a speaker. In 1984, a friend started a business called Nursing Support Services. I went to work for her for about one year, and was then recruited by Harriet Tubman's Battered Women's Shelter to be their executive director. I was there for five years. When I started, it was a fledgling advocacy organization. People had lots of really great ideas about consensus building and collective decision making, and plenty of insights about the need men often feel to be in control. But some of those same kinds of power and control issues were present inside the women's movement itself. This was not acceptable to me. I saw that some women of European heritage did not view African American women as equals. I wanted the center to reflect what Harriet Tubman was all about. I wanted her spirit to be happy that we were named Harriet Tubman.

We eventually got those things worked out, put in place organizational budgets, job descriptions, and performance appraisals, and defined the relationships between the board of directors, the executive director, and the broader community. Abused women who came into the shelter needed to understand that if they came in as victims only to take advantage of the system, they were doing the same thing that they were pretending to run away from. Being the executive director was tough, because it meant that in addition to fighting the world beyond our door, I had to deal with voices inside the organization that would determine what kind of organization we would become. One of the most helpful voices on the board was that of Rip Rapson, who later became deputy mayor of Minneapolis under Mayor Don Fraser. However, at this time, he was still with the Leonard, Street & Deinard law firm.

Rip Rapson and Don Fraser were active with Jim Renier and his work with Success by Six and Way to Grow. These organizations dealt with school readiness and the early developmental needs of children. In 1990 I was recruited to implement Way to Grow. It was a great experience. The concept was excellent, but I had concerns about the way it was going to be rolled out into the community. I wanted to insure that the community had ownership of the program, and that Way to Grow respected the culture of the community. This was my major contribution. Within five years, we were in six communities, and it was wonderful. Don Fraser fully understood what I was trying to do and was great to work with. Gaining the confidence of the people in the community was essential, and Mayor Fraser was so widely respected that we were able to gain the community's trust in a relatively short time. It was Don Fraser much more than the United Way or Jim Ranier, as well intentioned as they were, that helped bring the community to the table.

At some point, Way to Grow's success in these six communities brought along with it political pressure and resistance that began to impede our progress. One of the key corporate sponsors I helped recruit was Medica Health Plan. Jim Eland of Medica had hired Mike Christenson to be the executive director of their foundation. Mike became part of my community/corporate adoption project, and was incredibly helpful. The terms of the "adoption" required philanthropists and community leaders to join us on retreats, at which they had a chance to dialogue with regular people from the neighborhoods. At some point, Mike challenged me to get into the issues of infant mortality and the chronic diseases experienced particularly by African Americans. He and I put together a Healthy Powderhorn model by which groups in the community would work together to try to define what really caused chronic diseases. Then in partnership with the community, we would put together programs to identify and implement solutions.

I took two years and $600,000 from Medica, and moved from the executive director of Way to Grow to become executive director of Healthy Powderhorn. This became the Powderhorn Phillips Cultural Wellness Center. My ideas about having to start with one's self to create positive change in the community came into play with this new opportunity. The Cultural Wellness Center is a place where people learn about themselves, and put that knowledge into action to take care of themselves. People come here in crisis situations and we work with them, encouraging them to ask themselves, "What was my role in getting me into this situation?" We are teaching that we control our own destiny, and we can change any situation, not always individually, but as a people and as a community.

We do support groups, healing circles, and anything that helps people understand the concept and practice of community. In every culture, there are systems that give people meaning and hope. Somewhere along the line, many of us lost contact with those systems. There are ways that every culture gives its members the capacity to love, nurture, produce, create, and give birth. We have created self-study classes for groups, individuals, and cultures, to expose these capacities. We ask every individual that walks through our door to suspend their beliefs about race, economic status, political standing, and anything else that sets them apart from the rest of the world. We then invite them to look at their own people, their heritage and history, and ask: "How did we make it, and what were the resiliency factors that have kept us going?" Once you get to that point, then you can talk about the part those factors play in health and/or economics. From that point we can ask what kind of educational and employment systems they would want to have, now that they have a better understanding of themselves.

We really believe that as we grow and become more successful, others will come to understand how important this notion of cultural heritage and self-awareness is. The experience we are giving people is not just about pain or suffering, or even rational analysis. It's about how to walk in a way that brings peace, or how to build relationships in a way that establishes shared peace. We teach people how to implement, organize, and live in a beloved community.

One of the techniques we use is to have our participants sit with elders and tap into their knowledge and experience. Each cultural group has elders, or a system to connect with older people and learn about the decisions that guided them through life. Don Fraser served as an elder to many of the people we work with. His personality, which is much like that of my father, is the prototype we counsel for people who have experienced anger and abuse. Don Fraser has earned the right to be trusted and, through his experiences, has learned to relate to a wide range of folks in need of mentoring.

We hope to develop many more such role models through our educational systems. We also want to teach people like me—in their 60s and older—what it means to be an effective elder. We have people in their 80s who are learning to be elders. These are untapped teachers in the wisdom-practice of sharing resources, living together and nurturing peaceful relationships. Elders hold the wisdom that can help people commit to moving forward.

For generational continuity, we at the Cultural Wellness Center teach grandmothers how to be grandmothers, how to be part of the safety net in the community, so that the child protection system doesn't get involved and take the children. We teach them how to organize. I was here until late last night with a large group of people who were singing and talking and crying about what is happening to our children. That's the grandmother's group. Grandmothering is not about blood lines, but about teaching children in the community about discipline and love. To some degree, some of the time, we take back the church's role to protect, build, and nurture the spirit. The church can't do it alone, nor can the health care system or corporations do it alone. The community and the family have to be core nurturers of our young people.

I am working with Mike Temali of the Neighborhood Development Center as he does economic development and entrepreneur training. He has trained more than eight hundred African American entrepreneurs. Now that we have teamed up, we are seeing the largest number of African Americans ever start their own business. We teach the soft skills, the human development, and he teaches the hard technical skills of business management. This is a very powerful team approach. What's really behind getting a job is the question of how to live a life in such a way that you will always have a job!

We do ceremonies, rituals, and dinners. We have birthing teams that put young women in touch with their womanhood and the responsibility that goes with being an effective mom. We don't let them pretend that there is no responsibility involved with birthing and raising a child, or feel they can go to the larger system and have it take care of them and their child. What we teach is that you have to take care of yourself! It's part of that process of getting in touch with who you are and taking responsibility for your own actions.

The Powderhorn Phillips Cultural Wellness Center initially served the Phillips and Powderhorn neighborhoods. What we realized quickly was that people are not as attached to geography as they are to the nurturing relationships, life memories, and experiences they have. Now people come from all over to reconnect with culturally-based relationships. This whole thing about race and the practices of segregation that went on for years is still in the minds and hearts of people. African Americans and Native Americans describe no longer having a great attachment to geography per se. They have a lot more attachment to their families and cultural roots. We think that if we can get people back in touch with their roots, then they can make their geography work for them. We have created a theory of sickness that says individualism, loss of culture, and loss of community makes you sick. If you are alone and isolated, you can't build and protect yourself or your community. You have got to participate in the mainstream or in economic development. Culture is not something that separates you, but a heritage that pulls you together, and allows each one to exchange ideas and trade goods and services.

One of the places I would like to go is to South Africa. I want to explore how the indigenous people felt about coming together with those who injured them and took so much from them. My guess is that their beliefs are similar to the ones my father held. My father's living legacy gives me faith that we can do well, that people here will come to an understanding of who they are with their own collective spiritual vision, and become obligated to work together with other people. In other words, not to do to other people what has been done to us, not to hold people down because we have been held down, and not to be stingy because we have been shortchanged and deprived in the past. I think that is what the Cultural Wellness Center is all about. It's about both geography and spirituality as a place. It's about culture and politics. We see the religious and educational communities as our allies. They cannot and must not try to do the healing and teaching alone.

We talk about unleashing the power of citizens to heal themselves and build community. You don't do one without the other. If we are in a healing state, we are giving back. If we are not giving back, we are selfish, and we are going to continue to have the sickness we call victimization.

I want to continue to demonstrate that we can convert destructive behavior into something very positive. We need to grow our financial support and other resources, so we can expand these learning experiences. What is most difficult is proving that we are in fact producing the outcomes that everybody is looking for. Such outcomes—families sticking together and children holding their heads up high—take a long time to emerge, and are hard to quantify. We shouldn't have to pay for that with philanthropic dollars. I would like for us to get resources from institutions in the educational, governmental, and business communities who see it as in their enlightened self interest to invest in human development and beloved community engagement. I envision a group of institutions who can justify paying us, knowing that without our work, part of their work will not get done.

What an incredible difference it would make if a healing process that helps cure an attitude of victimization could be inoculated in all of us. As we were finalizing this book, Atum added this conclusion to her story.

This year (2008) I celebrate 65 years of life. My amazing husband of 18 years, my six children. five grandchildren and one great-grandchild are the gifts which have made my life so very sweet. With the beliefs, values, customs, knowledge, heritage and spirituality of black culture, I see a hope-filled horizon before me. This hope is due to an understanding of the role of my parents, grandparents, and others who've gone before me.

Thus, the circle of life continues, and makes us whole. Atum Azzahir is an African American woman blessed with parents who taught her both firmness and forgiveness in a way that allowed her to understand and minister to that sickness called victimization that comes to her people from decades of racism and physical abuse. She teaches us how to live together in dignity. What a blessing that is in these troubled times.

HOANG
K. TRAN

*I*n the end, regardless of our status, we cannot take *anything with us, so what matters is what we have left behind. Our work in social services is one way to leave good deeds behind. We help those people that share the same destiny with us. They don't need to know who is helping them, but I am sure that someone else is always looking over our shoulders.*

– Hoang K. Tran, May 2006

I first met Hoang Tran in his office on the second floor of the old Traders Market on Franklin Avenue in south Minneapolis. It was a beautiful spring day in May 2006, and we were at the offices of the Southeast Asian Refugee Committee Home (SEARCH), a rapidly growing organization that has had enormous impact on the lives of Asian Americans. As we sat in Tran's simple office, I literally forgot where I was as we traced his journey from Vietnam to France and finally to the United States. There is a spiritual quality to Hoang that puts one fully at ease as he relates the enormous challenges he and his family have faced. He is quick to say that there was divine intervention each step of the way as he worked his way through a maze of obstacles on his path to freedom.

Tran formed SEARCH in 1992. His goal was to create an organization that would assist low-income Southeast Asian refugees primarily from Cambodia, Laos, and Vietnam, including the Hmong, to become self-sufficient, to integrate into American society, and to contribute to the social and economic well-being of the community. The growth of SEARCH reflects Minnesota's role as one of the country's fastest-growing centers of Southeast Asian immigration.

People across the United States ask, "Why Minnesota?" In part, the answer relates to our longstanding record of outreach and missionary work, led by the Catholic and Lutheran communities. Their skill and success in attracting refugees to Minnesota is rooted in the very early history of our state. Minnesota also has demonstrated an interest in international affairs disproportionate to its size and position in the center of North America. The University of Minnesota has been at the forefront of this effort, and the late Governor Harold Stassen was an early advocate of the United Nations. In 1945 he was involved in drafting and signing its charter in San Francisco. Our leading grain and flour milling companies were highly active in world markets as early as the 1870s.

Hoang Tran's journey from Vietnam to Minnesota and successful efforts at empowering other Southeast Asians reminds us of the tremendous gift immigrants have made and continue to make to our economy and culture. It is redemptive for the United States to have the benefit of his great talent.

Hoang speaks slowly, as if some greater power is working through him. Each phrase is carefully thought out and articulated. His eyes twinkle as he describes the many hands that reached out to him along the way. He is a student of history, and his recall of events and dates is remarkable, as is his ability to relate the significance of one event to another that took place years later. This comes through clearly as he discusses the impact of corruption in his country, and how that, together with the drive for power, had nearly as much to do with the fall of his government as did the communist influence from the north. This story sheds light on the events leading up to the Vietnam War and the challenges for survival faced by those who are part of the elite educated class. Hoang Tran believes a higher power has shaped his life. He refers to it as "my destiny." This interview required two separate visits, and as I left, I regretted that there wasn't time for a third.

I was born in a small village in the south of Vietnam in 1943. My father was the mayor of that village. When I was six years old, I had to leave to go to another town named Tao to school, because there was no school in my village. The old school had been destroyed during the revolution against the French. At that time, leaving was the only way for me to get an education, so I went with my sister. My small village named An My is about five kilometers from the province of Binjou in the southeast of the country. This was very close to Bin Duong where there was a very fierce battle between the government in the south and the communist forces when they invaded South Vietnam. My village was only three miles from Tao, but there was no means of communication or transportation. My sister was living in Tao, and I moved in with her. I think I only spent two years living with my parents after that, except when I got tuberculosis in 1953. Already in my family, two aunts had died from tuberculosis. So I was lucky enough to get the drug Streptomycin and move back with my parents for two years until I recovered. I returned to finish primary school with my sister, and then entered middle school after completing the entrance tests.

Tao was in the city of Phu Cuong. This middle school was in another village on National Route 13. I went there for another four years. I can say that I was a good student. In high school in Vietnam we were able to choose between mathematics, science, or literature. However, literature was not available in any village near us, so I went to Saigon, the capital, to study literature. I finished my three years of high school in 1963.

For the most part, I had to make these decisions on my own, as my father had to leave the village when the communists came.

This was a revolutionary force supposedly to oppose the French, but in fact they tried to kill all the people that were working in the village. My father could not help me. He was the eldest son of my grandparents, who had a small grocery store in An My. My grandfather died at an early age so my grandmother had to take care of the family, including my father and five other siblings. Therefore, while my father finished elementary school, he was not able to go on to college. The reason I selected the program in literature was because that was the only way to get to Saigon. There, I was able to receive a better education. I studied French and English. Students were only permitted to study abroad if they were proficient in a foreign language. To study abroad was the dream of every student.

I am the youngest of ten children, the baby of the family. When I went to school in Saigon, my father did give me some money for my education, but that was about all he could do. I think it was my uncle who helped my father financially. He had studied in Paris and received a doctoral degree from the Sorbonne. Later he went back to Saigon as chief of staff for the last king of Vietnam. He was a rich man so he could be helpful to my father.

When I finished high school, I started my first job. I applied to be a high school teacher. I worked in one of the schools built by my uncle. In An My, with only two thousand people, my uncle built a elementary school, a high school and an agricultural college. He asked my father to be the supervisor of construction for the elementary and high school projects. It was the first high school in the village.

My uncle was working with the Republic of South Vietnam at that time. He was a very close friend of the brother of the first president of the republic, Diem Dinh Ngo. His brother Nhu Dinh Ngo was chief of the security and an advisor to the president. My uncle was the elected representative from our province. On November 1, 1963, Diem Dinh Ngo was subjected to a coup d'etat. Ngo was killed on November 2. I remember that very clearly because in America three weeks after that, President Kennedy was assassinated on November 22, a day I will never forget in my life. Vietnam was not secure. My uncle was sent to jail for fifteen months after the assassination. It was the soldiers that led the coup that sent him to prison. It was all about money, and the expectation that my uncle would pay them off. However, he had spent most of his money doing social services for the people, so he could not pay them off.

The reason why there was this revolution was that when Diem came back to South Vietnam to be the prime minister for Bao Di, he then turned against the king and dethroned him. Diem then established the first Republic of Vietnam. He had been living in the United States with strong sponsorship by Cardinal Spellman. His brother had become a priest, but there were not many Christians in Vietnam.

Diem tried to promote Christianity so that his brother could be appointed a cardinal. Diem was so aggressive that when roads were built, they would go around the Christian church but then force the Buddhist temple to be moved. This gave the military a religious reason to organize a coup d'etat because well over 90 percent of South Vietnam was Buddhist. That would not have been successful without intervention from America. President Kennedy was alive at the time and had sent Henry Cabot Lodge over as ambassador. Lodge developed a close working relationship with the soldiers. Most of the generals were trained in the war with the French. They were not well educated. So when they led the coup d'etat, they could kill President Diem and his brother but they had no idea of how to run the country. That was one of the reasons why, years later, we lost South Vietnam. In my opinion, while the military in 1963 was corrupt, they were not as corrupt as the then-communist regime in Vietnam. The problem was that they were not very smart, and continued to accept payoffs from influential people. My uncle had no group behind him, so that was why he was singled out and sent to jail. Again, that is why I never have been involved in politics in South Vietnam or in America. Some friends have encouraged me, but I want nothing to do with politics.

The role of Cardinal Spellman in promoting the Vietnam War is carefully spelled out in a book by James Carroll called An American Requiem. Carroll, a former priest, suggests that Spellman viewed the coming conflict as an opportunity for the Catholic Church to expand its influence in Southeast Asia. I recall that my own very early feelings were typical of many Americans, who viewed with alarm the possibility that all of Southeast Asia would be lost to communism. Only a few American leaders such as Senator Eugene McCarthy and Congressman Donald Fraser, both from Minnesota, pointed out that we risked getting involved in a civil war with a government in the south that was neither truly democratic nor fully supported by the peasant population. Many of us had done our homework by 1968 and our views changed dramatically.

I am very grateful to my uncle. He is ninety-five years old now, and living in Paris. When I wanted to become a teacher, my uncle was very helpful. The government was very particular about who could teach. My uncle was very powerful, and he made it possible for me to teach. He knew key people in the Department of Education. He was the one who recommended that I become a teacher after I finished high school. My dream was to teach in my home village, where I knew the people and they knew me. I wanted to help the younger generation in my village become more educated. They were as poor as I was when I was growing up, and I wanted to help them become better educated. I still have connections with many of the students, and have sent scholarships back over the years.

I was teaching at An My high school and at the same time enrolled at the university in Saigon. I enrolled in two faculties, the faculty of letters, which was literature, and the faculty of law. At the same time I was teaching 10 to 15 hours a week. I finished my law school in 1967 and went to work with my uncle, while at the same time teaching at the high school until 1971. Then I opened my law practice. We were still the Republic of Vietnam at that time. I was still practicing law with my uncle when the communists took over on April 30, 1975.

They did not take revenge against my family because of our good reputation in the village through many generations and the many students who appreciated my uncle's work and mine with them. My oldest brother had been killed during the war against the French. My other two brothers were officers in the army of the Republic of South Vietnam. They wound up being sent to re-education camps. Because of their service as military in the Republic of Vietnam armed forces, I was exempt from the military to stay home and take care of my parents. My mother passed away in December 2004 at the age of 100. My father passed away in 1972.

When the communists took over in April 1975, I was still in my village. They would not let me leave the country. I was jobless from 1975 to 1980. It was not until June 1980 that I received a visa to go to France.

I always have believed in the destiny of my life and the supreme God. That is, when we do good things, we will receive blessings back, not necessarily by the same people, but at some time in our lives. There is always some kind of divine God to help us. So I have believed that no one would cause harm to me or destroy me if I do the right things with my life. I am Buddhist. I don't know how to describe it, but I do believe that there is some kind of invisible connection that we call destiny.

When I had tuberculosis, my father took me to the doctor. He drew a picture of my lungs with black ink. He told my father that there was nothing he could do, and to take me home to die. However, my right lung diaphragm was very strong, and that lung recovered. When the communists came, the only reason one could have for leaving the country was for a medical problem. Because I could demonstrate a respiratory insufficiency, I was allowed to leave. They made me go before a special committee to get permission. In effect, they concluded that I was useless, neither a threat nor potential asset for the regime. Thanks to my uncle and his children, I had a sponsor and was admitted to France.

How my uncle was allowed to leave is inspiring. He was a rich man, with three villas and part-ownership of a bank in South Vietnam. He was able to leave, but was not able to get his money out. The communists almost placed him in jail because of his involvement with the Republic of Vietnam. However, he knew Ho Chi Minh from his studies in France. Ho Chi Minh used him as an interpreter at the peace conference at Fontainebleau in 1946. He saved the picture that was taken at that time with Ho Chi Minh, and so the communists left him in peace. When he arrived in France, he had no money. The lesson he later spoke of was that no matter how rich you might become, you can never keep it forever. Over his lifetime in Vietnam, he invested in many social service projects. He helped others with much of what he had accumulated. He helped raise my sister, and she became like his adopted child. He also had a servant that he adopted as his daughter when he went to France. He was able to bring them to France as family members, and they in turn were able to help him reestablish himself in France. The French welcomed him like a citizen because of their earlier involvement with Vietnam.

The communists left me alone because I had not worked for the government. As a lawyer, I was not rich, but had made a decent living. We had a two-story house with two cars. My wife had a driver, and we had two cooks in our house. Life was very good for us at that time. It was almost impossible to determine prior to 1975 which villagers were communists. Many later turned out to be supporters of the communists. However, in Vietnam, family and village relationships are very important, and with the exception of a few who betrayed their friends, most villagers respected our family and our role in trying to improve life in An My. My wife was a lawyer, and I met her in the court house in the summer of 1968. We married on April 30, 1972. It was exactly three years after that that the Communists took over. For our whole generation of intellectuals in the south, we lost everything, including our hope for a future in our country. We had to sell our cars and many household possessions, but we were able to keep our home. My sister-in-law lost her home. My wife's older brother had been a military judge, but managed to leave the country the very day the Communists took over. My wife's name was Nga Thi Nguyen. We wanted to have children. We prayed and prayed, and finally in 1979 she became pregnant. At the time I had applied for a visa to leave Vietnam. But I think the circumstances were such that destiny again was present.

I got a visa in December 1979, but they said it was only for me, not my wife. I explained that I needed someone to take care of me because of my respiratory problem. At last, after many prayers, we were granted a visa. Initially we tried to gain admission to Canada. With a visa, we could go to any country that would admit us. The Canadian official would not permit us to come because of my wife's pregnancy and the fear that she could have trouble in transit with no help available. Fortunately, my cousin in France had applied for a visa for us with the French government, and that was approved. We went home and my wife delivered our baby, our only daughter, in 1980. When my daughter was three months old, we left Vietnam for France and arrived June 26, 1980. We were not allowed to bring anything except $10 per person. When we were at the Saigon airport with $20 in our pocket, we were so happy to be leaving that we celebrated and spent $2 for two cans of Coke. We spent another $10 at Charles de Gaulle airport in Paris!

We were in the air for 21 hours non-stop from Saigon to Paris. Because my daughter was premature, we could not use normal milk, and my wife had to breast feed her along the way. So when we arrived in Paris, we purchased the special Nestle milk for my daughter and cigarettes for me. (Now I have quit smoking, and head a group of Asians promoting non-smoking.) We walked out of the airport with $8, wondering if anyone would pick us up. As it turned out, we were welcomed by the people working for the Croix Rouge, the French Red Cross. They asked us if we had a place to stay. We said that we did not. They welcomed us to follow them.

However, in the lobby of the airport, we did finally find our relatives. The confusion came from the lack of good communications between Saigon and Paris. I kept the remaining $8 for five years, until we came to America.

Life was not easy for Hoang and his wife in Paris. Work was difficult to find. Hoang took what was available, starting as a delivery person and then moving on after an introduction by friends to becoming an accountant for Marks & Spencer, a British retailer. He and his wife both enrolled in law schoosl, and Hoang became certified to practice law again in 1984. Despite gaining a prestigious appointment with the bar association in Paris, Hoang had his sights set on emmigrating to the United States. After all he had been through, he wanted to settle in a country where there was no chance of a communist takeover.

We came to Minnesota on September 25, 1985. How we made this move is quite interesting. In 1981, my wife's brother became a United States citizen. He applied and became a sponsor for us. It took four years for us to receive the invitation from the U.S. embassy in Paris. My wife had become a lawyer in France, and felt that we had both been working too hard. She felt that starting all over again in a new country would be too much for us. My argument was that we were both lawyers in Vietnam, and had lost everything except our memories when we left. My wife's father, sister, and brother were in Minnesota. Other than our cousin, our daughter would grow up without relatives nearby, and my wife would have family at a great distance, if we stayed in France. If we moved to Minnesota, we would have her family nearby.

When we came to this country, I had no worry in my mind at all. I was much richer than when we came to France. We had enough money to buy the airline tickets and get started here, at least for the first few months. The family helped us with the first month's rent, which was about $500. With a referral from my brother-in-law, I made $500 in October acting as an interpreter for the Toro Company, which was hosting a large international conference. That helped pay the next month's rent. Upon arrival, I went to the University of Minnesota to apply for law school. What I didn't know was that law school had already started. However, I did meet Marilyn Dean, the director of admissions. Her husband has an art gallery on Hennepin and 28th Street, the Dean Gallery. She helped me get an introduction to Robert Stein, the dean of the law school. They were so kind and treated me like I was one of their relatives. They admitted me to the University of Minnesota the following spring.

When I visited the library at the university, I met the director, a Japanese man. He gave me the address for the Center for Asian and Pacific Islanders, CAPI for short. I went there in October and at the time, there was a coincidence that the director, Mark Maggio, was applying for a job as administrator for the district court in Scott County. We talked, and he agreed to hire me as an employment counselor. I started there in November 1985, less than two months after coming to Minnesota. So I now had the money to pay for everything we needed.

In December of that year, the board of CAPI organized a committee to recruit a new executive director, because Mr. Maggio had gotten the Scott County job. There were eighteen applicants. I was appointed executive director in February 1986. That agency had almost no money at the time, and was employing eight people plus myself. My first job was to find the dollars to keep the organization going. Our first grant came from Nancy Latimer at the McKnight Foundation. Then Duane Scribner of the Dayton Hudson Foundation approved a grant to us. Next came a grant from Bruce Palmer at Northern States Power Company. We continued later to get support from John Pacheco at the power company. It was like there was some sort of divine intervention when this funding arrived. I was new to Minnesota and was not familiar with the foundation community and how things worked.

Hoang's initial funding sources illustrate the effectiveness of the Twin Cities' funding community. These donors were bright, sensitive people who likely remembered their own roots, and had the vision to recognize the value that Asian refugees could bring to our community. Over and over again, leaders in business and the foundation community have reached out and taken risks to support prospective social entrepreneurs who had the vision, skill and passion to make their organizations work. In many cases there was no organizational track record, so a bet had to be made about the prospective grantee's ability. Hoang proved to be a very good bet.

I think one of the reasons I was successful was that I dealt with people from my heart, and they in turn dealt with me from their hearts. One of the things that made me very happy was the food shelf we set up at CAPI, which helped over 3,000 people each year. In the non-profit sector, the only thing I could really demonstrate to others was my sincerity. I did not know how to write a proposal. However, I was lucky to have as a friend Irene Long, who was familiar with this process and worked for Pillsbury United Neighborhood Services. In 1986 the budget for CAPI was $186,000 with eight employees. By 1992 we had twenty-five employees and a budget that exceeded $700,000, with a surplus of $300,000 in cash. We also had in process a community center campaign that had raised $500,000 in cash with an additional $500,000 committed. Thanks to funders like General Mills, the McKnight Foundation, Dayton Hudson Foundation, the Saint Paul Companies, the Otto Bremer Foundation and others, we did buy a $500,000 building in the Seward Neighborhood in Minneapolis in November 1991.

All of this was done, I believe, because I dealt with people from my heart. I finished law school in 1988. Only in America can one work like this and serve people while earning a living and going to law school at the same time! So I was a full-time executive director, a full-time law student and at night a babysitter, so my wife could go to William Mitchell Law School. She got her degree in 1990.

In July 1992, I walked out of CAPI. In a way, I was a victim of my own success. I believed that CAPI could be home to a wide range of Southeast Asians, but this proved to be extremely difficult. There were many differences between several of our constituencies. I felt good about my work. CAPI now owned its own building, had 25 employees and $300,000 in the bank. Several former board members and I immediately founded SEARCH (Southeast Asian Refugee Community Home.) There was the publisher of the Asian American Press, the president of the Vietnamese American Community, the president of the Cambodian American Association, Irene Long, and me.

My wife at the time was working on her own, in space provided by the Taylor law firm. So once again I found myself out of work. That same month, in July 1992, I rented our first law office in the TCF tower. My wife agreed that we could use the law office space to start SEARCH. So I started the process of writing up the documents for 501(c)(3) status, the bylaws and other documentation to start this new organization. Our first grant, $25,000, came from Hennepin County Department of Employment Assistance for employment programs. The McKnight Foundation responded with a grant for $30,000. Michael O'Keefe and Nancy Latimer were so very helpful. I will never forget these people. When we Asians say we are grateful, it is not for two minutes. It is for life! The Minneapolis Foundation followed with a grant of $20,000 from Donald Drake. In October 1993, we rented a small office at 1421 Park Avenue and SEARCH had its own location.

My philosophy is that if we help others, some other people will help us, and we never lose. By working in social services, we will never be lost. If you do some good things for someone, some others will help you. That is why I have survived. After starting in France with eight dollars, now, twenty-six years later, I have a good life, and my daughter is now a lawyer.

After I opened my law office in August, my wife was diagnosed with breast cancer in September of 1992. We struggled with that for three years, and then on August 5, 1995, she passed away. This, of course, was very difficult for me. SEARCH faced severe financial problems, and at the same time, my wife died. For the first time, I felt that I might surrender. So in 1995 and 1996, I had to wave my salary. Fortunately, I still had my law office. I am not too superstitious, but one night, I saw my late wife in a dream and I prayed that she would help me deal with the survival of SEARCH. I saw her smiling, and the following day, and for weeks afterward, when I came to SEARCH, I received more and more funding. I believe that my wife helped me fulfill one of the dreams I had when I came to this country. That was to help others so that we could help ourselves at least morally, psychologically, and for our own well-being.

In late 1996 we began to have contact with the broader community of Minneapolis. One of my good friends who was very helpful, though he has now passed away, was Gleason Glover of the Minneapolis Urban League. Another close friend was Yusef Mgeni of the Minneapolis Urban Coalition. The other very special friends were Nancy Latimer and Duane Scribner. I will be grateful to these friends for the rest of my life. In 1997 we received a grant for $50,000 over eighteen months from the United Way, and $5,000 from the Urban Coalition, thanks to Yusef Mgeni, for employment programs. In 1998 and 1999 we expanded our employment programs and secured more funding from a variety of sources.

By 2000, we had ten staff members and a budget of about $400,000. The collapse of the stock market reduced our funding in the following years, but we were conservative and had saved funds in the event of hard times. The Bush, Otto Bremer, and McKnight foundations continued to be helpful, and in 2004 we were able to add an additional staff person and move our offices to larger space at the Ancient Traders Market, off Franklin Avenue. At our current location, we are able to see many more clients and the parking is very good. In fact, in 2004, the board of directors authorized us to reach out to other ethnic groups, including African refugees. In 2005, we served 865 clients, of which we placed more than two-hundred in employment and many in day care training.

This year [2006] we now have twelve staff members, including two for the tobacco prevention and intervention program funded by Blue Cross Blue Shield and MPAAT. We are still very careful with our funds. We don't have a receptionist, and I do not have a secretary. Our administration and fundraising costs are less than 15 percent of our budget. This is so important, to show our funders that when we receive more money, it goes to help our clients. We do not deal with our clients as if they were beggars. We deal with them as individuals who need our services, and we do it with dignity and very professionally. I treat my staff the same way, with careful emphasis on their work skills and style in caring for others. In my twenty-one years of running non-profit organizations, I have never had to discharge anyone. I have told employees that if they do not believe in the goals of the organization, they can leave. It is my belief that if they do not do a good job with their work, sooner or later they will feel bad about themselves and leave on their own.

Working in the non-profit area is never easy, and many times it is not fun. But I can say that it is very rewarding, because we are working with our hearts and souls. If you do not show that you are useful to others and love other people, nobody will love you back and be helpful to you when you need them. That is a principle that I never forget: that if I do the right thing I will be rewarded, but if I do the wrong thing I will be punished, whether anyone else knows about that or not. So I do believe in some sort of God. My God is not Christ or Buddha, but something that is over all of these spiritual leaders.

In the end, regardless of our status, we cannot take anything with us, so what matters is what we have left behind. Our work in social services is one way to leave good deeds behind. After half a century, my old school in An My continues to produce many intellectuals who finished high school and become doctors, lawyers and professors. I am happy to say that over the last twenty years in this country, I think I have helped indirectly thousands and thousands of people. We help those people that share the same destiny with us. They don't need to know who is helping them, but I am sure that someone is always looking over our shoulders.

LAURA
WATERMAN
WITTSTOCK

My classmate from fourth grade whom I visited just this April is the same as me politically. Why did that happen? Why is our outlook so geared to looking at society as a resource, and looking at humanity as a very rich environment to be part of? How did we develop this thinking, that we don't want society to be so stratified and people to be so hardened and separated from one another?

– Laura Waterman Wittstock, July 2005

Laura Waterman Wittstock describes her round-about path to the Twin Cities and the founding of an American Indian news and journalism training service, MIGIZI, as "an example of serendipity personified." Granted, coincidence and luck played a role in her odyssey. But it's clear that Wittstock's own drive and ability were also key ingredients in establishing a non-profit provider of journalism training and news services to and for native people in the Upper Midwest.

Clearly an independent thinker, she owes much to the Hawaiian teacher who convinced her that she had great talent. School also exposed her to journalism and the skills required to "get a story right," while making it attractive to the reader. The writing career that followed prepared her to become a leader in the national American Indian Movement, which triggered other opportunities that eventually brought her from Washington D.C. to Minnesota.

We met in her home in northeast Minneapolis on a warm July afternoon in 2005. Laura knows herself well, and is at peace with a world that she knows is in need of healing. There is a reassuring tone to her voice as she discusses the challenges she sees ahead. She has been involved in the struggle for human rights for many years, and has been successful in convincing her friends in the Native American community that, by coming together with people of other cultures, real progress can be achieved, without sacrificing their own cherished cultural values.

Wittstock helped form MIGIZI in 1977, and became its second executive director. American Indian journalists and university students met in Minneapolis to form a not-for-profit enterprise to provide electronic communications know-how and services to the American Indian community of the Upper Midwest. In partnership with the American Indian community, MIGIZI teaches elementary, secondary and adult students to use the tools of communication. In addition, it offers a customized curriculum for upper-level elementary and middle-school students in technology, computers, math, and science. Recently MIGIZI began a new initiative in media training that promises to launch the organization into national prominence. More than forty Indian- owned television and radio stations now exist in the United States, and the Native American professional ranks in the communications field have grown exponentially, thanks to MIGIZI.

Laura's parents divorced when she was quite young, which may have instilled self-reliance and independence in her at an early age. That breakup was likely the reason her mother sent young Laura from upstate New York to Hawaii, which she feels was instrumental in developing her intellectual creativity, despite the heartache involved in leaving home. It is with her parents' break-up that her story begins.

When I was four, my parents separated. I was the youngest of five children, and my closest brother was ten years older. My siblings were fourteen, sixteen, eighteen, and twenty. It was a very unfortunate end of a marriage, and I was the only female child. Here was this custody battle, right at the end of World War II. Here is this little kid watching the VE Day parade coming down Niagara Avenue in Buffalo, New York, with all the buses, flags flying and horns honking, and she is saying to herself, "What the heck is going on?" I knew about rationing, because we had been careful about household supplies like sugar. I was a fairly naughty little kid, and would get one of my pals to forge my mother's signature at an Italian grocery store called Sinatra's. Then I would go into the store with the note and my best angelic look. The note would say something like, "Please give Laura Jean one dozen donuts." We would divide up the donuts, and at the end of the month when she got the bill, my mother would hit the roof. She always forgave me, though.

My oldest brother returned temporarily from Honolulu, where he had been at Pearl Harbor. He had been lucky on December 7, 1941, and was called out of the motor pool just before the bombs fell. He had married an Hawaiian. My mother had the idea of sending me with my brother to Hawaii in 1945, which was about as far away from my father as she could place me. That made my father very unhappy. My brother, his new Hawaiian wife, and I drove across the country to San Francisco, and got on one of the Matson Line pre-World War II cruise ships. It was three and a half days to Hawaii. I was incredibly seasick for the first two days. There were troops on the ship, and Halloween came during the crossing. I came back to our cabin from trick-or-treating with a sailor's hat full of dimes and nickels. When we got to Honolulu, we could still see strafing marks on the buildings and damage from the bombs.

The territory of Hawaii had about a 90 percent Japanese population. The Hawaiians were very much a minority in their own land, and among them, an American Indian was nothing more than a speck. I entered third grade. By the fifth grade, the territory decided that they would sort the students by giving them a battery of aptitude and IQ tests. Beginning in sixth grade, we were divided into A, B, C, and D groups based on these test results, none of which we were supposed to know about. Any kid could figure this out, because at one corner of your little student card was the letter number of your group, and at the other corner was your IQ. The school would suggest to those of us that were by genetics or luck in the A group that we were destined for great things. (As we know now in education theory, a child will usually perform up to the level of expectation.) I was also selected in the fifth grade by my teacher and my principal to submit some of my work to the National Education Journal, which is the old National Education Association teacher's journal. My elementary school principal gave me lessons in meter and rhyme, and they started to promote me to write skits and things, and to work with younger students on literary work.

By the time I got to seventh grade, I was pretty well tagged as a writer. One of the reasons I wrote poetry, at least I thought at the time, was that I was very lonely in my home, and felt that I was different from other kids. Feeling different is one of the hardest things for kids to deal with. For me, this was a burden, but for my teachers, it was a gift.

Once, in seventh grade, my teacher accused me of plagiarism. She picked up my poem, ripped it up and threw it in the trash. Several of my classmates stood up and told the teacher she was wrong. I get emotional today just thinking about that. Somehow the principal must have heard about this, and she came back and apologized to me. It just knocked me over, because in Hawaii there is the custom that the teacher is never wrong. The other side of that was that if the student failed, the teacher also failed. That's the Asian tradition. So for those kids to stand up and tell the teacher that she was wrong was revolutionary! That teacher later became a friend, and she was the first person from the school that my family invited to a birthday luau. Her name was Miss Huckstein. She was a German woman from the States, who obviously had grown up in a time when teaching was more formal. That lesson didn't completely overcome my feeling of being a fifth wheel. But I decided I could either use it as a positive experience or be ashamed of it, and I chose the former. The upside of all of that was that I learned that it is OK to be different, and the downside was that I developed a reserve that I never lost. There has always been a little reserve between me and other people.

My brother and his wife were very strict people who did not believe in extracurricular activities. They would not let me go out of the house alone until I was sixteen years old. Hawaiian society was very "old school," and did not have the concept of "teen age." You are a child, then an adult at sixteen, and there was no in between. After sixteen, you were invited ceremonially to eat with the adults. However, girls were still sheltered beyond that.

This kind of upbringing meant that I didn't go out and have a date until I was eighteen. This allowed me to focus on writing. I wrote the senior class song, pieces for pep rallies, articles for the school newspaper, and audio scripts. The high school principal decided that he wanted us to have a student radio station, so we re-wrote and read the daily news, produced a monthly play, and in effect became journalists. In 1952, when presidential candidate Dwight D. Eisenhower came to Hawaii, Republicans were using the slogan "I Like Ike," a phrase that means something totally different in Hawaiian, something not exactly flattering. Richard M. Nixon was the vice presidential candidate. He came to our school, and we interviewed him on our radio station. It was just amazing. We had that experience because we had been segregated, selected to be in this sort of special group. We were supposed to be leaders, and our teachers and advisors hammered on us to be all that we could be. This is one example of serendipity in my early years.

The second example deals with my being the only female child in our family. In Seneca society, identity is passed through the female side. It is matrilineal. Being the only female, my parents were very concerned that I grow up and carry on the family line. It was a very heavy burden because after my parents died, my older brothers leaned on me to sort out what to do next. Not so much the funeral arrangements, but more the issue, how does our family identity move forward?

My mother and father differed over which path I should take after high school. There were no Bureau of Indian Affairs scholarships in those days. There was no way to go to college unless you had means, and we did not. My mother would work a little bit, enough to pay for a class, and then I'd work some. My parents and my uncle were looking for the next generation to do something to escape poverty. Both of my parents urged me on.

However, at age nineteen, I fell in love, got married, and had five children, one after another. I had returned from Hawaii and gone to San Francisco State College at my mother's urging. In the meantime, I met my future husband, who was an engineer with Douglas Aircraft in San Francisco. They were building a new bomber, and his job was to guide the bomber to Jacksonville, Florida, its eventual home with the U.S. Navy. In Jacksonville and other communities we moved to, after the kids had gone to bed, I would spend my evenings writing stories and poems and sending them off, hoping they would be published. I would say that my writing at that time showed lots of energy, but not much expression. My children were raised as if they were little adults. I would read the paper, relay the news to them, and then ask them what they thought. They were my audience. Television in early 1960s was really awful. There wasn't a real breakthrough until Star Trek. That program wasn't about the future. It was about the present, and asked relevant questions about what we were then facing as a society.

During this time, mother would send me pictures and press clippings about the American Indian Alcatraz occupation in 1969. She had become president of the San Francisco Indian Center during the occupation. She was in charge of logistics, which meant getting blankets, water, and food to the island. She was right in the thick of all these changes going on with Indian affairs, while my father was still living on the reservation in Cattaraugus, New York, near Niagara Falls. They were still separated, and he was oblivious to all the changes going on. He was very quiet, very traditional, and given to an Indian way of life. They were as different as night and day. She had moved to San Francisco in 1946 because she wanted to get away and grow. It was a brave thing for an Indian woman to do.

"Relocation," as it was called, started in the mid 1950s, as Indians were enticed to move away from reservations. Dillon Meyer was hired by Franklin Roosevelt to run the Japanese internment camps in the United States during World War II. He seemed to like that type of work. After the war, he was named commissioner of the Bureau of Indian Affairs. The first plan he developed was to move Indians off reservations and into cities, with the thought that they would "lose their way back home." It was a plan for permanent relocation. His hope was that they would assimilate into white society.

It was a disastrous plan, and extremely painful for those Indian families that were separated. Soon, reactions started. If a member of a tribe moved to San Francisco, got sick, and died, the relatives on the reservation would want the body to come back home and be placed with the rest of the family. People like my mother did what they knew how to do. They made quilts, potholders and anything they could think of, just to raise money to send bodies home. Relocation is what caused Indian centers to emerge all across the country. A place was needed where Indians could go, get help and meet other Indian people. Women like Emily Peake here in Minnesota with The Upper Midwest Indian Center came up through the same kind of social environment as my mother. American Indian women who had come out of the Depression were the backbone of the urban experience. These women, beacons in their own families and visionary in their own way, led the way for the American Indian Movement to happen. Without their work, we wouldn't have Indian centers today.

While we were in Jacksonville, my husband, who was ten years older than I, decided to become a Republican. As he became more conservative, our political views began to differ dramatically. I was part of the Committee for Nonviolent Action. The organization began in 1957 with peace protests against atomic testing. In Florida, I was able to take part in the 1963 Quebec to Cuba Walk, which was organized to build support for world disarmament. Bradford Lyttle, an organizer of the walk, visited me in my home. He was a very gentle person with willpower made of steel. I clearly remember how he guided me to decide to help, and then made a list of what I would pledge to do for the walk. It was not easy to do, with children to care for. My husband bitterly opposed my involvement, claiming that I was a threat to his high security clearance. I had other things to be concerned about as well. Some of the walkers were beaten and jailed in Atlanta, Georgia. Because of a U.S. ban on travel to Cuba, the marchers ended the walk in Miami.

I contributed to the CNVA Everyman catamaran project in the early 1960s as it prepared to sail into the U.S. atomic testing area in the South Pacific. The objective was to disrupt the U.S. "Dominic" high altitude nuclear testing. This project had a handful of wealthy contributors, but most were people like myself, who only could give small monthly amounts. Prior to that, I was a supporter of longshoremen labor leader Harry Bridges, and of Gus Hall, a leader of the Communist Party USA, who was from the Iron Range. I was a great admirer of these agents for social change. In an odd way, I also admired some of the good stuff that Jimmy Hoffa did, with his populist approach to unionizing the workplace. People like Harry Truman represented strong and compassionate leadership to me, as did John F. Kennedy, aside from his order to continue nuclear testing.

My husband and I separated and divorced. I then met a young college student, Lloyd Wittstock, just out of graduate school. He had completed a Ford Foundation fellowship, and was teaching at an African Methodist Episcopal College in Jacksonville. He was like a lot of people from the Upper Midwest who had come south at about the time of the 1960s freedom riders. His home was Sheboygan, Wisconsin. Black colleges were desperate for faculty, and he was one of those very bright twenty-five-year-old professors being

heavily recruited. We met at a political meeting while I was working with the African American community on economic and social
oppression. There was no American Indian community to speak of
in Jacksonville, so I joined a group of African American Democrats.
With them I worked on the Humphrey presidential campaign in
1968. Lloyd and I decided in 1970 that we were right for each other,
which was remarkable because I was thirty-two, with five children,
and seven years Lloyd's senior. Then an opportunity to leave Florida
came along, and Lloyd went to teach at Federal City College, a land
grant institution in Washington D.C. I arrived a few months later,
and we were married in a little hippie barefoot wedding, with a
Unitarian minister and five children standing around.

My father advised me to go to work at the Bureau of Indian
Affairs in Washington, D.C. My mother responded, "Over my
dead body. You can't go to work for them, when you are opposed
to what the Bureau of Indian Affairs stands for." I had no leads,
but had worked as a copy writer, and had a fairly good portfolio
to take with me. The Hecht Company, a large department store
chain in Washington D.C., hired me and put me in charge of all
suburban store advertising. The job paid well, but I could have
done it in my sleep.

Then I met Jim Thomas, a public relations entrepreneur from
Alaska. He was Tlingit Indian. He had been with the National Congress of American Indians, the largest organization serving American Indians in the country. Jim said, "Boy, have I got a job for you!"
There was a brand new magazine starting up called the Legislative
Review to report on legislation affecting American Indians. He took
me to the office, and I was hired right away, but as a staff assistant. I
had never done secretarial work, so I didn't know how to put people
on hold or any of that. I was hanging up on them and showing
myself to be totally incompetent. So the boss had me write down
the number and short title of all the Indian related legislative bills.
I had a long list of bills to write down. It was sort of like copying
the telephone book. In 1970, in a Congress of two years, there were
about twelve thousand bills. Of those, about 10 percent impacted

American Indians. There was a prominent American Indian attorney called F. Browning Pipestem. He and Edgar Cahn wrote a book in 1970 called *Our Brother's Keeper: The Indian in White America*. This was an update to the Brookings Institute report on the status of Indian administration in 1928. I had never met him, but Browning Pipestem apparently had heard about my past work, because he came in and asked to see my boss. He was an imposing four-hundred pound man. Ten minutes later, he came out of my boss's office and said, "You are now the editor of the *Legislative Review*!" I realized at once that I had been given a huge opportunity, and one on which I had better deliver.

I served as editor for three years, during the occupation of the Bureau of Indian Affairs, and during consideration of critical new legislation, including the Alaska Claims Settlement Act and the American Indian Education Act. There were a host of executive orders, including the restoration of Blue Lake to the Taos Indians. We can say what we will about Richard Nixon, about his person and character. There is a huge shadow over his name, but he firmly believed in the traditional Republican position of states' rights and Indian nations' rights. He set in motion the most liberal agenda of self-government for American Indian tribes in 150 years. This was enormous, and he got very little credit for it. This was not easy for him, as he had just won re-election in 1972 and had a full plate of second-term goals. Though he had won re-election by a landslide, thousands of people were marching in the streets against the Vietnam War. I marched with my four year-old child in a stroller, and was nearly run over by a Washington, D.C. police officer on a motor scooter.

All of that turmoil was preceded by the creation of the American Indian Embassy in Washington D.C. and the citizen's arrest of John Old Crow in 1971. Old Crow had been an ineffective bureaucrat in the Bureau of Indian Affairs, and AIM performed a citizen's arrest on him for some of the same reasons we see today; neglect, being lied to, and mismanagement. The slow burn against government dereliction of duty had been building since the late 1950s. However, the "Caravan of Broken Treaties" happened during Nixon's re-election campaign. So in my dual role, as a reporter on call with the American Indian Press Association as well as editor of the Legislative Review, I spent six days inside the Bureau of Indian Affairs during the occupation. There was a lack of sanitation and food, but we were told if we left, we could not return. At the very same time, the National Tribal Chairman's Association was being formed in Eugene, Oregon. Our four reporters were split: two of us in D.C. and two in Oregon. We two thought the other two reporters were lucky, but we were wrong.

There was a lot going on, and it was enormously exciting. Reporters were coming from all over the world to cover these events. Nixon was sequestered in the White House. The Indian leaders Dennis Banks, Clyde Bellecourt, Hank Adams, and Russell Means were devising tactics, and some were meeting with Nixon aides Leonard Garment and Harrison Loesch to forge a peaceful way out of the occupation. A major objective was to win agreement on the "Twenty Points Position Paper" authored by Hank Adams, an activist out of Washington State. I was reporting and trying to keep up with all of this, and in an interesting way, following the destiny my mother had laid out for me. Had I gone to work for the Bureau of Indian Affairs, I might have seen this situation very differently.

But the Legislative Review folded for lack of funds in 1973. Wittstock, out of work, came to the Twin Cities to write a newsletter for the convention of the National Indian Education Association. She thought it would be a short-term assignment. She was wrong. Many of us who have been in positions that require recruiting new professionals to the Twin Cities know that while convincing someone to move here is often a great challenge, once that person is here and settled, it takes an act of the Almighty to get him or her to leave.

Upon arrival in Minneapolis, I was recruited to become the National Indian Education Association's full-time staff. I told them that my husband Lloyd was still teaching at Federal City College in Washington D.C., which made the decision very difficult for me. My future boss, Kiowa educator Herschel Sahmaunt, said, "Well, I will hire him too!" My reputation had preceded me as this iconoclastic journalist with leanings toward the American Indian Movement, but not so biased that I couldn't be objective and credible.

My job was brand new, and involved going to fledgling schools like the Red School House and Heart of the Earth and learning what they were doing, to see if we could make them laboratory schools and improve their situation. I was met with some skepticism by the local Indian community, who felt they had done pretty well before this new kid from the East arrived. It was a very different experience for Lloyd and me, because we were both looking at ways to improve opportunities for this diaspora of urban American Indians. There were lots of Indians getting more education in the post-World War II environment, with the GI Bill and changing attitudes about what school means. Our role was to be catalysts for change. It was very exciting, but it was probably painful for the children. They didn't get to see mom and dad very much. We were working very long hours.

We had parties at our house every weekend. These parties were to generate ideas. People would sit around the table and argue about Indian politics, education reform, Indian identity, and tribal politics. It was a coffeehouse setting and a hotbed for ideas, with everybody wanting to talk at the same time. The presumption was that we were the generation that was going to do something about all these problems. Now, in our late sixties, we look back and ask, "Where did we get this idea that all of this was going to be our job?" Back then, no one wanted to be viewed as the leader, and the format was informal, cooperative, and collegial. In fact, there would be subtle ridicule if someone was viewed as positioning himself as leader. While people can surface as leaders in the national arena, at the local level, Indian people will get up and leave when you boldly say, "I have a plan!"

My move to Minnesota is another example of serendipity. My boss had known of my previous work. In addition to writing for the

Indian Press Association, I had edited a special edition of the Legislative Review on the BIA occupation. Requests for the publication had come from all over the country. My boss felt that Minnesota was a very special place and fertile ground, and that more things were possible here than in some other places where Indians live. He was right about that, but being a catalyst and actually establishing a reputation of trust was way more difficult than we ever imagined. The new schools, Heart of the Earth, the Red School House, and other Indian organizations had their own ideas. This was the age of silos, where organizationally, you had to define yourself uniquely. Tough individualism was the best survival strategy an organization had. Foundations in those days were not really looking at collaboration, cooperation, and partnership. They wanted to know how you were different. Indians have a natural propensity to collaborate and group together, so to become silos was difficult. That prevented the National Indian Education Association from being the catalyst that could help these organizations. We didn't have the financial resources to get things done quickly. With gentle persuasion and by offering new ideas, we made a difference, but it took a long time. My lapses into "reporter mode" made people suspicious, so I had to learn to stifle my natural curiosity and my journalist's skepticism.

I did eventually go to work for the Red School House for three years, and wrote some of their programs and the national models they instituted. About the same time my colleague Elaine Salinas, who later succeeded me at MIGIZI Communications, and I wrote the model for White Earth Circle of Life School. That school is still going. Elizabeth Whiteman Runs Him and I wrote the Indian teacher training program at Hamline University, and that went on for ten years. Elaine and I met again at Heart of the Earth School, where we co-ran the school, took it to its first $1 million budget and accreditation, started the basketball teams, gave the teams a name and developed the small learning community idea. This was back in 1985, before Bill Gates came along with his small school approach. We called it a school within a school, and it was for the kids that were smart, had issues, and needed to have somebody sitting around a table with them to get them excited about learning. It was so successful that other kids were trying to fail their classes, so they could get into the school within a school.

I kept my hand in writing, as much as I had time for. While I was still at NIEA, Scott Raymond, Margaret Peake Raymond's son, came to me with his idea. Indian students at the University of Minnesota were reading the news over KUOM. This harkened right back to my high school experience. There was no Indian news at the time, so they decided to do it themselves. Roger Buffalohead, the first chairman of the Department of Indian Studies, encouraged them, along with Andy Marlow, a Dakota Indian at KUOM. They had students reading a five-minute news cast. That was just one little station at one university. We asked ourselves if we couldn't do more. We got the small group of Twin Cities Indian journalists together with students, and the idea surfaced that we should start MIGIZI Communications. This was the mid to late 1970s, when the country was having an economic downturn, and corporations were cutting back their spending on advertising. One half of the Indian newspapers in the country went under!

In 1977, when we formed MIGIZI, we decided that print was not going to be our medium. Radio was cheaper. It was going to be our medium! Only a tiny number of tribes had radio stations, so we decided that we would rely on the college and university radio network. Getting started was very difficult. Mick Anselmo was general manager at KSJN on Lilac Drive in Golden Valley, and he took our show. It was called "A Native American Program." There was a little music and some talk, including interviews with people. It was a commercial station, not a public station. We became known as a favorite during the "truck driver hours" of 2 a.m. to 4 a.m. From that, we spread out. At the time, Minnesota Public Radio had no interest in us. Staff there sneeringly called us "Me Radio." We returned the favor by dubbing them "The Klingons." We did get a number of college stations, but public stations were the key.

Serendipity again stepped in. The federal government had a program in the late 1970s that allowed tribes to buy towers and stations. They started buying into FM spectrum and created tribally-owned stations on reservations. There are now about forty tribally-owned stations across the country, a pitiable number that may be doubled in the new FM spectrum sale. MIGIZI, with a volunteer staff at the beginning, really pioneered this entire movement. We operated out of a building on Franklin and Bloomington, right in the heart of Indian country in Minneapolis.

In 1979, there was a blow up on the Red Lake Reservation. There was a shooting and a burning near former Chairman Roger Jourdain's property. Jourdain's firing of an employee had sparked the trouble. There was a riot, and they closed all the roads. We taped a sign on the side of my van that said NEWS and went up there. In those days, reporting equipment consisted of a tape recorder and alligator clips. If you could get to a public telephone and clip on the clips attached to the tape recorder, you could get your story to the stations. It was very primitive, but we were there, on the spot with the news. It was very interesting and exciting. There were also Minnehaha County jail riots in Sioux Falls, South Dakota, and other trials in the region. To the extent we could drive and cover those stories, we did.

The Division of Indian Work for the Greater Minneapolis Council of Churches was run by a very independent Dakota woman, Vernell Wabasha. She would give us gas money, and pay for supplies and some tables and chairs. She so believed in freedom of the press and the establishment of the American Indian press that she did whatever she could to help struggling little MIGIZI Communications produce the news. She was just wonderful. Her husband is the eighth generation of the Wabasha line, which goes back to American Revolutionary War times.

Soon we had a steady stream of people coming to our office from all over the region. We were the only organization of its kind around. Jim Lenfestey came when they first began to publish *The Circle*. It's a monthly American Indian news magazine based in the Twin Cities. That has been the history of MIGIZI for twenty-seven years. We were this different animal in the non-profit community, which made foundations and corporate philanthropy scratch their heads and ask what box they should put us in.

One who never asked us that question was Russ Ewald at the McKnight Foundation. He got it right away. He always treated me in a very avuncular fashion, almost as if I were family. He was very instructive, and gave advice to me freely. I would prepare ahead of time, and write down bulleted points describing what we were doing and what we needed, on one sheet of paper. He could glance at that, and then he knew what I would be talking about. The funding world was small at that time. Russ, Jim Shannon, Tom Beach, and Jerry Falk were all at the Minneapolis Foundation at one time or another. Bill Humphrey was at General Mills and Dick Conte and later Duane Scribner were at Dayton's. Our funders were The Minneapolis Foundation, General Mills, Honeywell, Dayton's, The McKnight Foundation, and The Campaign for Human Development out of the Minneapolis/St. Paul Archdiocese, as well as the National Indian Lutheran Board in Chicago. The Lutheran Board leader was Eugene Crawford. I met him through my work in Washington D.C. and sent him a letter about MIGIZI. He sent us $1,000, which paid for an entire year's rent, and it bought us the precious tape that we needed for reporting. We were ecstatic. That was a huge contribution for us when we were just getting started. Other funders came along after that. The foundations must have talked to each other, because each funded different parts of our operation to get us launched. Finally, the Campaign for Human Development came along with a grant of $30,000, which really helped get us launched. These were people who were not afraid to take risks.

It is different today, with foundation staff operating in a more structured environment. These early foundation leaders came out of liberal arts and business backgrounds, and they relied on their intuition and knowledge of the broader community. If you came to them, looked them in the eye, told your story and it rang true, you got your money. Of course, the deal was, you had to perform and not screw things up. We had a lot of pressure on us, but there was no question that we were going to do well and meet the expectations of our supporters. I regret that young people today are not living in the tough love environment that we were living in then. As pre-baby boomers, our generation has a lot in common with these younger people, but we had richer opportunities than these post-baby boomers are finding now.

As a group of students and journalists, we decided early on that we would always have community service as part of what we do. We would always work with other Indian organizations in some way. We would find opportunities to use our skills to tell their stories. We did slide shows for Little Earth, and a Honeywell slide show for the American Indian Opportunity Center on job skill training. John Bolger, president of Bolger Printing, and David Nasby, program officer at General Mills, helped us with these. We did newsletters. We started a television program called Madagimo on Sunday mornings. We also did a KFAI-FM weekly radio show. This was a new community station that started when MIGIZI did. At one time we shared the same one-room office in the basement of Heart of the Earth School. At our peak in 1985, we were producing tapes that were mailed out to about fifty stations all over the country. We were doing local television, radio, and promotional print work for non-profit agencies. In the meantime, Lloyd worked first for St. Mary's College, then Hamline University, and then, starting in 1983, the American Indian Opportunities Industrialization Center. He is still there. He and I, along with Elaine Salinas, worked on securing the initial funding for the AIOIC in 1980. AIOIC was founded in 1979 but did not begin operations until 1981.

Meanwhile MIGIZI continued to develop training partnerships with the University of Minnesota so that we could move more Indians into journalism. There had been a national Civil Rights Commission report in 1974 called "Window Dressing on the Set." It was a wake-up call. If you looked at the pieces on the pie chart, you could see the slices of the share of Native American, African and Asian communities in media employment. The sliver for Indians was barely visible! There were almost no Indians in journalism. That motivated us to start working with the journalism school at the University of Minnesota, and we got some federal money. The internship training we provided was in radio production, radio management, and journalism. So they got practical production and management training while they were going to school, and it was fabulous. The interns were paid $400 a month, which was a lot of money in those days. Jerry Kline was the head of the School of Journalism at the time. The tenured professors would not allow him to give credit to our internship students, even though Jerry wanted to. Today, that is not such a problem. One of our first interns was Hattie Kauffman, who went on to CBS and became a national television journalist. She is still on the air. We are so proud of her, and proud that she came out of MIGIZI.

My philosophy is that you hire the very best you can find, and then you let them come up with new ideas and see what happens. Then you work together to learn and teach, and that's a give-and-take process, full of risks but a lot of fun. One of the big learning experiences we had when the federal training funds for interns was cut in 1982 was that we couldn't go back to the foundations and ask them to start us up again. It was extremely frustrating. The Indian Education Act was ten years old. We asked ourselves, why couldn't we work with high school kids? Why couldn't we broaden our reach to do broader communications training? No matter what you are going to do in life, you will always want to learn to write, improve your verbal skills, use a camera or recorder, interview people and learn how to do research. So we did a survey of high school teachers and counselors, their students and parents. They said yes, they would benefit from a communications-based after-school curriculum. We then wrote a request under the Indian Education Act and it got funded. In 1983 we asked Roger Buffalohead to experiment with a curriculum. We bought our first computers, which were primitive in those days. We could sense immediately that this was going to be something big. We called it "Achievement through Communications," and added educators to the staff. The mission of MIGIZI was expanded to not just get the news out, but invest in the future of Indian kids. The students would produce newsletters, videos, and audios, and would appear on programs. Occasionally we would have them do a story for our syndicated news program. With this program, they learned to take charge of their own education. By high school, we learned that the participation of parents drops dramatically. We initially recruited at South High, Heart of the Earth, and then Roosevelt. We had to move off Franklin Avenue to Cedar and 24th Street, and then in 1986 to our present location, at 31st Avenue and East Lake Street. There was initial resistance by the board in moving out of the Phillips neighborhood, which was home to so many Indian families. But as predicted, the Indian population has expanded east into the Longfellow neighborhood. MIGIZI now owns half of the block on the north side of Lake Street.

Being able to serve high school students was a big step forward for us. The program is now called Native Academy, a division of MIGIZI. It continues to do radio, television, and promotional work, and our budget is over $1 million a year. A very high quality staff is still a hallmark of the organization. All of our objectives have been met, with the exception of spreading out regionally and nationally. I am convinced that the staff, under Elaine Salinas's leadership, can make that happen.

I retired as head of MIGIZI Communications on December 31, 2004. It was the right time for me to move on. That month, I gave a luncheon at Mai Village in St. Paul for the entire staff and former staff members. It was wonderful, but five days later, I nearly collapsed with a terrible pain in my side. I was having trouble breathing. Since I am the driver in our family, I drove myself to the hospital. They did a CT scan, and found that I had pneumonia. One month later my kidneys failed, and I was hospitalized again. I said to myself, "Wow, you do all these years of work, and then just drop off the face of the earth." It was a real turning point for me.

The first thing I thought was that I wanted to live to see my grandchildren get older. One is three, two are nine, one is ten and the oldest is twenty-seven. My oldest son is an engineer with a three-year-old daughter and lives in Virginia, near Dulles Airport. My second son is married, designs electrical systems for large yachts and things, and lives near Virginia Beach. My youngest son lives in the Twin Cities with his partner, and is an artist and works at a company that does shipping. My oldest daughter works at MIGIZI, and is a teacher with a specialty in math and computer science. My second daughter is a choreographer, and has a health background and does physical therapy. My goal in retiring was to be able to do my work, write my books and do things with our grandchildren, especially travel. They love to travel.

I received excellent care in the hospital, but that consumed the first three months of 2005. Now it is July, and I have only had a few months to sort things out. I am going for my first election to the Minneapolis Library Board, as I was appointed by the mayor for my first term, and he asked me to stand for election this time. I told Mayor R.T. Rybak that I had never run for public office in my life and he said, "You should do it. It will be fun." I told him: If I win and you win, you can appoint someone else to the board. If I win and you lose, I'm still on the library board. If I lose and you win, you can still appoint me! So, I said, that's a good deal!

I still do a little consulting work for MIGIZI, but have nothing to do with the management. I am a firm believer that when you decide to retire, you should walk out the door and give your successor a free hand to do the job his or her way. I was there twenty-seven years, and I am not one to want to get founder's disease.

One of the key lessons I have learned is that you can never underestimate the value of a good marriage. I think Lloyd and I took that for granted at the start. Success really is having that ability to know one another, and be able to argue in a way that is passionate but not angry, and to do that in a respectful and constructive manner. We still get angry, that's a given. But we also quickly forget. Lloyd and I have quite varied interests, and we are very different people. We live in the house together, and whatever staying power we have had these thirty-five years is sort of a combination of being able to tolerate each other's foolishness and to accept each other's differences, while having that strong loyalty to one another that transcends sexual attraction.

The other thing is that I have very old friendships. Some go back to elementary school; others go back thirty or forty years. When we visit, we don't feel any different inside of these bodies that warp with age and time than we did as kids. In many ways we are still kids. Our long-term friendships run very deep.

My old friend Gary Fife just visited from Alaska. His wife's mother had died, and they only had a few hours in the city before their plane was to leave. He was the first person I ever hired. He was a young journalist, a Cherokee-Choctaw from Oklahoma. I hired him again when he moved to Minnesota to become MIGIZI's first executive director. He brought me a beautiful necklace made of blister pearl to commemorate my retirement. We had only a few hours to talk about what we were doing with our lives, but it was as if he were living next door. The time went by so quickly, and then he had to leave. It was such a good feeling to affirm that our friendship is solid and deep.

Michael Dalby, another friend, just came through brain surgery. He was MIGIZI's first engineer and he is part of our family. We met when he was in graduate school at the University of Minnesota in 1979 and we have been as close as non-kin mother and son could be. You just can't underestimate the anchor you get from these long-term friendships. These friends will tell you if they think you are doing something that is not true to your character, and that is the most valuable thing about them. No bullshit.

This is a good time of life for me. There are a number of books I am writing. One is fiction and involves a little Dakota girl with special powers. I'm also writing some Dakota history. Older age has turned out to be a far more active period of life that I ever could have imagined. There is just so much to do. I plan to be an eternal student.

Lloyd and Laura have a remarkable spirit that has allowed them both to survive, prosper and make enormous contributions to their community despite adversity and set backs. They recently shared with me that they had lost their oldest son to cancer on

July 9, 2007. It was a crushing blow to the entire family, which came at the end of a two-year struggle. The cancer was diagnosed at about the time of our original interview. They feel that their lives "have been profoundly changed, and they find reflection a more welcoming exercise than ever before."

JOE ERRIGO

*What we do has to make sense to liberals,
conservatives, middle-of-the-roaders, people of
all faiths, and maybe most importantly, young people.
So I believe one of our greatest challenges is finding
and developing the individuals who will be our
future leaders during times of accelerating change and
increased diversity.*

— Joe Errigo, July 2005

He didn't get the job he wanted, so instead he started something
new. It became another one of those Minnesota miracles that
is recognized as a national model. Common Bond Communities has become the largest provider of affordable housing in the
Upper Midwest. The organization serves more than 6,000 residents, including 1,500 children. It has more than 4,000 units of
housing located in 68 properties in Greater Minnesota, the Twin
Cities and Wisconsin. Common Bond says its mission is "to build
communities by creating affordable housing as a stepping stone
to success."

Errigo pioneered the notion of adding supportive services to
large multi-unit affordable housing complexes. They would include
self-sufficiency support for senior citizens, which postpones nursing
home care; early childhood learning for pre-schoolers; English as a

second language for new immigrants; computer training and career placement for new and returning applicants to the job market, as well as a host of health care support services that make many costly emergency room visits unnecessary. He served as Common Bond's executive director for 25 years, from its founding in 1981 until his retirement in December 2006.

When I met Errigo in his office, in the shadow of St. Paul's majestic cathedral, it was clear that he was excited about telling his story. It was obvious that he had reflected on his life many times in the past, fitting the impact of his early years to later events much like fitting together pieces of a jigsaw puzzle. There is a restlessness about him as he speaks, as if he is afraid that he will forget something if he doesn't move forward quickly. He speaks proudly of the social values of his parents, which from his early years gave him insight into racism and the behavioral changes that are best suited to avoid being part of sidestepping that problem. His parents also taught Joe to think independently and develop empathy for people who differed from what was then considered mainstream society.

Joe Errigo is the very personification of a social entrepreneur. He could have become a brilliant architect, but instead applied those skills to surviving the politics of the Catholic Church and spearheading an effort to provide affordable housing in conjunction with the supportive services that truly empower residents.

Joe has been honored publicly as a social entrepreneur, standing on the platform with leaders from the for-profit business community. He has demonstrated that rare combination of a successful businessman's social and managerial skills and a good architect's attention to detail. Here is Joe's story, as he related it on July 19, 2005.

My parents probably had as much to do with developing my social awareness as anyone. They helped me see early on the importance of caring about people who were not like us and were not doing so well. My dad was a public sort of guy who did a lot of good work in the community.

The entrepreneurial part of my skill set was explained to me a few years ago when a management consultant came in with tests that looked at characteristics such as motivation. We were looking for an operations manager, so to try out his technique, we had him test another guy on our staff and myself. He asked you to identify things in your life that motivated you, and then prioritize them. So I put down things like how I used to sit down in the middle of the living room as a child and build something out of blocks. I think I told him that I did it there so I could be noticed by everyone. He concluded that I needed to get up out of bed in the morning with a challenge, and it has to have a social purpose. That was probably as good a definition of what motivates me as any. I couldn't just get up in the morning and make widgets with the idea of selling more than the next person. That part of me was built into my thinking since I was a kid.

My sister was four years older, and in our early years we weren't allowed to go to the Rialto Theater in Wilmington, Delaware, where I grew up, because the Rialto in the 1950s didn't allow black people to go there. My cousin used to tease my sister and say, "Oh Mary, it's all right. You don't have to worry about that, because you're not black." My old man laid down the law. We weren't allowed to go to a place like that. At the time it was sort of annoying, because the other kids could go, though I did understand his point of view. But it was many years later that I truly appreciated the value of all of that. You could go, turn your head and wink, and say it's a bad thing, but the point is, you are still paying money to get in. That is one of my earliest recollections of sorting that kind of stuff out, and deciding what was important and what wasn't. That theme kept recurring as I grew up in the 1960s.

My parents were both first-generation Americans. All four of my grandparents were born in Italy. I knew them. This whole generation of immigrants, they were truly "Old World" folks. They helped me understand what real struggle looks like. My mother's mother never learned to read or write, but she did memorize the telephone numbers so she could dial her seven kids. My mother was the second oldest and my dad was an only child. He never knew his real dad. The grandfather I knew was his stepfather, ten years younger than my grandmother, which some of the old generation thought was scandalous. My parents made great efforts to show that they were true and successful Americans. I never was forced to learn Italian as a kid. Later on my dad would tease me about not learning Italian. If they had pushed me, I would have, but they never really pushed. I think they wanted me to adapt to the new ways. However, my dad was active in the Sons of Italy, a big national group. He was an officer and became one of the governors. My mom during the 1940s and 1950s was a pretty standard stay-at-home housewife. She had worked for a long time before she got married, and years later, when my dad was out of the picture, she went back to work, telling me, "I worked hard years ago, and I can do it again!" They were pretty self-sufficient and intent on succeeding with the American dream.

The themes of social justice, racial equality and service to the disadvantaged were woven through my early years. My dad was the first Italian admitted to the bar in Delaware. That was in 1929. He went to the University of Pennsylvania and graduated in the class of 1925 and then went to law school at Penn. The idea of being a groundbreaker was built into him. In my dad's law practice, he brought in a partner named Sidney Clark who was African American. He might have been the first black admitted to the bar in Delaware. He later became the first black judge in Delaware. There was always something that was brewing around social justice issues that Dad would take a stand on. He was a volunteer for a group that served physically handicapped people. He brought me along, and I would observe people with muscular dystrophy and that sort of thing. Of course, he did that on purpose. It was easy in those days to be disconnected from anything that was a problem, but fortunately, I got connected.

We were able to travel a lot. We traveled sometimes with the Lion's Club, as my dad was a member. When I was four years old, we traveled cross-country by train to a Lion's convention in California. It was a fabulous trip. I was notorious on this trip because I had this stomach disease as a kid called celiac, which meant I couldn't eat fats. I was eating a ton of bananas because I couldn't digest fatty foods. I became known as "the banana boy!" Four years later, we visited St. Anne de Beaupre Church in Canada, famed for its miracles such as people leaving their crutches behind. The only thing there to eat was a ham sandwich from a street vendor. My parents watched me eat it without having a stomach seizure, and proclaimed that St. Anne had performed another miracle!

The other famous event of my childhood was passing out on Pike's Peak in Colorado. I never made it to the top, but recovered on the way down. The experience with celiac gave me a sense of what it is like to be different from other kids who could eat whatever they wished. Overall, my early years were very happy ones, but somehow I got the idea that I had to push hard to be successful.

When I was a freshman in high school, I worked in Dad's office running errands, and was able to watch how he worked. He was defending some guy in a trial one day that he knew when he was a kid. The guy was accused of drunk driving. At the end of the day, he got him off. I asked him about the verdict, and he just said everyone is entitled to a defense. The following summer, I'm working in the office again and the same guy gets hit with the same charge. This time he was driving a pickup truck across somebody's lawn. My dad must have done this masterful job, because he got him off again! The judge called my dad up to the stand afterwards and said, "Joe, if I ever get caught for drunk driving, I want you to defend me." I told him that this guy sure sounded guilty to me, and that I don't understand this bit about everyone being entitled to a fair defense. I couldn't believe how this guy had gotten off driving across someone's lawn and almost killing a baby. That was my introduction to the criminal justice system, and this whole thing about defending a guy who was guilty. Nice theory, but that was probably the main reason I didn't go into law.

When I was looking to decide what field I would study when

I went to college, Dad introduced me to two friends. One was a banker and the other an architect. So I went see the banker with his starched collar and three-piece suit. He showed me around the bank, and I said, "That's very interesting" and such. Then I went to see the architect. He is an Italian guy named Leon Fagnani, just a marvel of a guy, kind of a Renaissance person. He was an old-school designer and visionary, and liked to beat the hell out of contractors. He was a fun sort of guy. So there were these two powerful career images, and I just couldn't go the banking route. I wound up working for Fagnani during college. He was a real renegade, and taught me a lot about moving the system along and how you get it to work for you. He let me do working drawings. Right in the middle of my work, he pulled me away from the drafting table and we went out to the school, where I could see the windows I had sketched being placed in the walls. He said, "You have to not just draw, but get out on the job and make sure it's done right. You can't let these contractors get ahead of you, and if you gave them an inch, they'll take a mile." That was terrific experience for me, and it paid off big time for me in later life.

There was a pastor in my parish named Roberto Balducelli. He was a fiery little priest who built the parish. He went to all the Italian contractors and got them to donate time, and if they didn't, he would blackball them. He put the church together and the school at a bargain price, and he is still at it today. So I got exposed to a lot of people who thought and worked outside the box.

One day at lunchtime, I stopped at the local tavern and bought my first drink. I was old enough at the time. I came home boasting about it. My dad didn't chew me out. He asked me, "What do you suppose Leon Fagnani would say if you came back from lunch with alcohol on your breath? Just think about it." Did I ever! And what really made the impression was that he didn't say, "Don't do it." Instead, he got me to visualize the consequences. Those folks in those days had a way of getting the message out without rubbing your nose in it. They knew how to teach.

My dad was a real piece of work. One of my mom's buddies

when she was a kid, Rose Bernardo, said that he was always a dreamer and didn't keep both feet on the ground. Most of the time I think he did. Years later I read a book about the Italians by a guy named Luigi Barzini. In his view, Italian culture mostly had to do with the celebratory nature of life. It celebrates sad and celebrates happy and celebrates everything else. There is a kind of denial in Italian culture that anything is ever wrong. When I read that book, it occurred to me that it described my father exactly.

I have no idea what kind of money my dad made, but having a second child really stretched their financial resources. In 1953, he was appointed commissioner of public safety in Wilmington, heading the police and fire departments. In the early 1960s, he was appointed to a restructured version of the same position, public safety commissioner. Even though he was a Democrat, the then-mayor recognized Joe Errigo as a bipartisan and effective public servant with the image of "Mr. Clean." He enjoyed the job a great deal, and would write letters critical of FBI involvement in local law enforcement matters. It was clear that he gave a lot of his time away to civic issues, at the likely expense of his law practice.

At age 22, I was in my fifth year of a five-year undergraduate architecture program, working on my design thesis, which was a prison, of all things. The guy next to me was working on a mental institution, signs of things to come. One day I got a call from my brother-in-law to come home, because my dad was in some real trouble. I had no idea what that meant. It turned out that he had left town and was on the run, and there was a warrant out for his arrest. I didn't know anything about it. I was at Catholic University in Washington D.C., and drove up to Wilmington. When I went in the house, my mother was distraught, with all the relatives standing around. Nobody knew where he was, and the warrant and his disappearance were all over the news. He called a day later, and I answered the phone. He said someone recognized him, and he'd been picked up by the police in Elkton, Maryland. So the Wilmington police chief, who worked for him, and my brother-in-law and I went down and picked him up. Somebody figured out that the best thing to do was to take him to the Delaware State Hospital, our mental institution, and have him committed. That was a smart move politically and legally. It was also a powerful scene for me. I still remember sitting next to my dad in the lobby, this guy who was a giant in my life, and saying to him, "Dad, it's going to be all right." He was then 63. That was March 1966, and he stayed at the mental institution three months. He was released in June and allowed to come to my graduation, and then the trial was set for July. The night before the trial, we walked around the block together, and he stopped and turned to me and told me that tomorrow he was probably going to jail. Even then I still imagined that this couldn't be happening—that there was some magic that would lift this burden off our backs.

He was sentenced to five years, and wound up serving a year and a half, mostly in a minimum security facility in Dover, where we visited him a lot. His initial months were spent in the maximum security facility in New Castle County, which was very hard on him because, as he said, a lot of the people there he had helped "put away." The warden was the same guy my dad had sent me to for help with my thesis. Technically, he had been found guilty of forgery and embezzlement. The judge that sentenced him was a lifelong friend of my dad's, and said, "This is really distasteful for me, Joe, but I gotta do what I gotta do." My dad even wrote a book in prison dealing with his whole experience, of course changing the names. It wasn't exactly a best seller! Cousin Lou Borelli helped finance the publication of dad's book. Dad had given Lou a camera when Lou was 15. Years later Lou opened up the most successful full-line camera shop in the state. Dad really got him started.

When my father got into trouble, there was a letter to the editor written by an African American woman that said, "Let us not be too quick to judge Joseph Errigo, as he has done a lot of good things for the underdog." I'd like to be remembered the same way. When I later talked to my dad's two law partners, they told me that the amazing thing was that my dad kept meticulous records of every transaction. It was clear, they said, that he wasn't hiding the transactions, and intended to eventually repay the accounts. It was all on this pink pad in the top drawer of his desk. The borrowed funds totaled something like $400,000, big bucks in those days.

Everything he had was put into a receivership, including the house. They then sold off investments and real estate to satisfy the debt, and my mother went back to work. The whole thing is so interesting because my dad never lived high on the hog or drove Cadillacs or anything like that. But it was a shock. Everything we had was gone, and we were getting handouts from cousins, a hundred dollars here and a hundred there, just to buy groceries.

Seeing his respected father publicly recognized as a law-breaker must have had a profound influence on Joe Errigo. Questions of family economic survival and his own ability to envision a future free from the shadow of this sad event must have weighed heavily on his mind. Most of us face the role reversal of children parenting their parents much later in life. In Joe's case, it hit him at that critical point when he was in college and preparing to chart his own course in the world. My guess is that this episode drove home to Joe an understanding that we are all fragile and vulnerable, that heroes can fall, but also that with the support of family and friends, redemption and reconciliation can take place. Common Bond Community's incredible success reflects these same values.

Georgiann and I were married while my dad was in prison. We had met at Catholic University in Washington D.C., and married in 1967. If I had stayed around Wilmington, I could probably have had things handed to me. I didn't want that. I worked for Fagnani the first three years I was in college. In my fourth and fifth year I worked for an architect in Washington, and then when I was accepted to graduate school, I asked my mom if she wanted me to stay in the Wilmington area. Dad was still in prison at the time. That was when she reminded me that she had worked for several years before she got married, and that she could take care of herself.

That was important because it showed me her spunk. Up to that time, she had been sort of quiet, like many women were in those days. But when times got tough, she rose to the occasion.

After the house was sold, she rented an apartment and got a job doing the books for Lou Borrelli at the camera shop. She did a fine job, and after my dad got out of prison, they moved to Dover to be out of Wilmington. It would have been tough to stick around. My dad got a job with a former state senator in Dover doing paralegal work, since he had been disbarred. He wound up running errands around the court house, and occasionally ran into the judge that sentenced him. He always got a kick out of that. He was on a mission to get reinstated to the bar. That's what he wanted to do before he died. He worked for several different people, and later when Pete DuPont was governor he applied for a pardon, and he got it! DuPont took all kinds of heat for it from the Republicans. The receivership had been paid off in full by then and he didn't need to go back to practicing law, but he was able to get his pardon. He died at 78, and so he lived about ten years after he got out of prison. My mom died of cancer in 1973, and my sister of cancer at age 44. My mother-in-law was the last to survive of the four grandparents. She survived burns over 35 percent of her body when her clothes caught fire bending over the stove at my home in St. Paul. That happened the same year that my mom died.

I went to graduate school at the University of North Carolina at Chapel Hill. My focus was on city planning. I got drafted twice during that first year, because Vietnam was heating up in 1967. The draft board back in Wilmington was after me, a guy named Colonel Hall. My dad had been on the draft board, and Colonel Hall went out of his way to pursue me so he wouldn't get accused of favoritism. In those days you could only get a deferment for the remaining months of the semester in which you were enrolled. When I got the second notice in North Carolina, I visited the draft board in Durham to find out what my options were. Georgiann and I were married by then, and she was pregnant with our first child. I wrote a letter to the draft board asking for a deferment. I didn't know it

at the time, but that was five days before they eliminated the deferment for being a father. I finally appealed my case to the head of
Selective Service. The long and short of it was that my son kept me
out of Vietnam. The guy sitting next to me in architecture school,
Jerry Costello, became a pilot and his name is on the last panel
of the memorial at the Mall in Washington D.C. I was so lucky
to have talked to the draft board in Durham because they were
required to tell me all the options, and Colonel Hall was not about
to explain them to me. The "good" colonel and Jerry's death probably turned me against the war more than anything else. I talked
earlier to Colonel Hall on the phone and told him I had a summer job in urban planning with HUD, the federal Department of
Housing and Urban Development, in Atlanta. This was during the
riots, when our cities were burning down. It was considered a critical occupation at the time. "Urban planning?" he says. "What in the
hell are you going to do with urban planning in Vietnam?" I began
to realize that so many guys in leadership positions were just plain
nuts. When I heard that, I really began listening to what was going
on in our country.

There was another guy who was a year behind me in school,
just a great guy and a super jock. He got drafted when he was in
city planning school in Rhode Island. He goes to Vietnam and is
standing on the side of a hill when his leg gets blasted with shrapnel
during an attack. I asked him whether he had any idea how bad the
war was when he first went over. He said, "I had no idea how whim-
sical it was whether you lived or died or became injured. If I had any
idea, I would have gone to Canada in a minute!" These things had
a major impact on my views.

Before 1967, I had not been particularly involved in the
debate or protests about the war. That year, things heated up
on campus, and North Carolina was just bubbling. There were
debates and protests against Dow Chemical for making napalm.
Vice President Hubert Humphrey came and spoke. There was this
classmate named Don Ridings, a wonderful guy who had been a
journalist with the *Charlotte Observer*. Don leaned over and told

me that Humphrey was one of the best politicians in America. I had never heard of him before! Humphrey spoke in defense of the war. Ted Kennedy came down to talk a few weeks later, and things really began to heat up with the student body. The intensity of the protest was so great. A lot of people got fired up in those days, and wound up getting involved in careers and forms of activism they had never thought about before. It's fascinating how many of those folks wound up running major organizations later. It was a terrific learning experience.

I applied some of the lessons of those years much later, when a young African American I had hired came in and asked if he could go out and organize in the black community. I said sure. A few weeks later, he wanted to organize people that were sexual minorities. I said yes again. One month later, he asked me if it was all right if he tried to organize a union among our employees. Of course, I said sure again. I asked our lawyer if this was a serious threat, and he assured me that it would only be a serious threat when someone pinned you against the wall uttering obscene invectives at you! So that era taught me tolerance. At the time, all of us seemed to be on earth just to challenge the system.

In my last year of graduate school I sent out letters for job interviews. I had an opportunity to interview in Atlanta and one in St. Paul. Ed Helfeld was the head of the HRA, Housing and Redevelopment Authority, in St. Paul. Helfeld was one of the urban renewal gurus of that era which included Chuck Krusell of Minneapolis and others across the country. I came to St. Paul for an interview the day after Martin Luther King was shot, April 5, 1968. When I came through Chicago, I could see the fire on the horizon. When I got to St. Paul, the HRA was closed.

Later that day, I got in and met Helfeld. He was really smooth. I had a professor in graduate school at North Carolina named Henry Hightower, a great professor, but he had a terrible stutter. You had to stick with him as he spoke. In the middle of the interview, Helfeld interrupted me and said, "You had Henry Hightower, didn't you?" I said yes. Shortly thereafter, he introduced me to Don

Cosgrove who was head of planning for the HRA. Cosgrove walked in the door and said, "Hi." He had a stutter just like Hightower! Helfeld had been trying to tell me ahead of time what was coming. I was so impressed with the way Helfeld handled that, without saying, "Before this guy comes in, let me tell you something." It was another one of those lessons learned. I worked for Cosgrove for three years. He designed the skyway system in St. Paul. One of the reasons I came to St. Paul was because I hadn't been here before. I looked at the map, and said, "That is way past Chicago, so maybe I should go there." I came to Minnesota never expecting to be here more that five years. Georgiann and I have raised two kids here. It's a great place. We have been here since 1968!

Three years after I started with the HRA, I got wind of a job that was with Father Ed Flahavan, a priest with the Archdiocese in St. Paul. His job was running the Urban Affairs Commission, the church's social justice department. He wanted to get into affordable housing. Flav was about 39 at the time. He was a friend of Reverend Harvey Egan, longtime pastor of St. Joan of Arc Catholic Church in Minneapolis, and a close friend of the late former Bishop Jim Shannon. Jim was Ed's role model. They loved to have fun together. In fact, the three of them got thrown out of a restaurant once for making too much noise. They were very close. It was through Ed Flahavan that I met Jim Shannon, and what a wonderful mentor that guy was.

This was a time of tension within the Catholic Church in the Twin Cities and for Archbishop John Roach as they sought to satisfy both the Vatican and the social needs of the community at the same time. Former Bishop Jim Shannon left the priesthood in 1969 after counseling a low-income woman with several children that he could not in good conscience advise her to abstain from birth control, as the Vatican required. Having been president of St. Thomas University and in line to become archbishop, this act of courage sent shock waves through the Minnesota church. Progressive parish leaders like Harvey Egan,

Ed Flahavan and others were encouraged. Some left the priesthood, while others remained and focused their energy on social
justice issues such as poverty and neighborhood redevelopment.
Joe Errigo arrived on the scene as the church was wrestling with
these incredibly tough issues.

I interviewed for the job of associate director of urban affairs with
the Urban Affairs Commission of the Archdiocese in St. Paul,
and somehow got the job. They assumed I knew something about
housing! That was in 1971. After a short time, it was clear that we
needed a separate corporation to do housing, or we would have
been too tight with the archdiocese. A priest who was on the commission would ask each year, "Do we really want to be in real estate?
The church has gotten into a lot of trouble in real estate." I would
respond by saying that we already were in real estate, and that there
were real people living there! We had already completed housing in
Red Wing and Northfield, of which I was very proud. We solved
that problem by setting up a separate corporation. The day I started,
April Fools' Day of 1971, I received a letter from Joe Gabler, then
the head of the FHA (Federal Housing Administration) local office.
That letter was the approval for our first two deals. So Joe Gabler
calls Ed Flahavan and says, "Hey, that new guy must be pretty
good!" Joe was a wonderful guy who made a huge difference as a
public servant.

Flav left in 1977 to take over St. Stephen's Church in south
Minneapolis and their social service operations. Apparently one of
the true tests of priestly achievement in the Catholic Church is running a parish, and it was Ed's time to make this move. He did a great
job there, getting the shelter started, serving meals to the poor, and
delivering a host of new services to poor folks. Four people applied
for Ed's job, including myself. I lost by one vote, and Jan Mathison
prevailed. On the way out the door that night, Dick Palen, who was
a successful contractor in town, turned to me and said, "Joe, this is
the best thing for you. Don't get tied down with church bureaucracy
and that sort of thing. Take this housing thing and really run with

it!" It was the best advice I could have had. I would have been on a church salary and been burdened forever with church politics if I had gotten that job. It was really a green light to take "the housing thing" and make something of it.

The day after the decision was made, Archbishop Roach called me at home and asked what had happened, and said he had thought it was going to be me. I told him, "So did a lot of others!" Not long afterward, I got his support to spin the "Community Development Corporation" out of the archdiocese, and we set up the current corporate structure. CDC became Westminster Corporation and later Common Bond.

One of my first board members, Frank Mullaney, and Ed Flahavan were the two people who had the most influence on me in what came next. Mullaney was a founder of both Control Data and Cray Research. He saw an entrepreneurial spark in me that I never knew I had. Mullaney was a classic entrepreneur, part of the group that originally bolted from Univac to start other companies. He was very wealthy, but so very down to earth. He would push me when we first set up the corporation to run it like a business.

Flav had been an incredible leader in my earlier job, but also gave me plenty of space to do my thing. He didn't have a modern management bone in his body, but he knew how to be a leader. He told me I could work 18 hours a day if I wished and burn myself out, or come up with a different routine. It took me a year to develop the right kind of balance to my job. It was really the first time someone else wasn't managing the daily calendar for me.

We got Westminster organized in the mid 1970s, and then in the 1980s had the greatest growth surge we had ever had. We took over Torre de San Miguel on St. Paul's West Side, and we were court-appointed receiver of Little Earth of United Tribes, the Indian-sponsored housing complex in south Minneapolis. We were doing all kinds of creative things and federal money was still flowing, but the end of that was in sight.

I went to a housing meeting in New York in 1973, and heard a minister from Riverside Church lamenting the fact that President

Nixon had impounded all the housing funds. I said to myself, that didn't make sense. How could you stop doing this work, just because the federal government had cut back its support? So in the mid 1970s we began limited partnership deals, such as Westminster Place. Mullaney was the person that made me figure out how to finance affordable housing after HUD cut back its funding.

Someone suggested we look at limited partnerships. I asked Mullaney about this, commenting that maybe this was just another way for the rich to get richer. In his creative way, he told me to go back and figure out whether we should do it. We had never set up a for-profit ownership entity. I told Frank that if we raised $350,000 from 19 limited partners, we could build five more handicapped units and put in an elevator. I noted that if we didn't attract housing investors, they'd just buy into other limited partnerships that owned cattle. Mullaney's response was, "All right."

The point is that he made me figure it out! He never told me how to do these deals. He just kept forcing me to figure it out on my own. It was a fascinating time in my life. If someone were to ask me what I would like on my tombstone, I would have it say, "We did it without the Archdiocese…..and we did it with the Archdiocese!" The proof of the pudding was when Monsignor Ambrose Hayden, whom the current Archdiocese building is named for, wrote me a note that said, "You are doing a marvelous job, Joe, in spite of the rest of us!" Hayden was the archdiocese's vicar general, or chief operating officer, the inside guy who would basically say that it was better to ask for forgiveness than to ask for permission. He encouraged me to go ahead and do a project, but not tell anyone about it until it was done. A few years later, he took me to dinner at an Italian restaurant and gave me his blessing for the Selby-Dale project. Of course, that just happened to be in his Cathedral parish! Hayden was the most unlikely suspect to support a guy like me. Yet Hayden was like Flav in some respects. They both liked to challenge the system they were part of.

Ed Flahavan, by the way, just got married, at age 74! He wrote to the Vatican, and was given permission to renounce his vows and get married. So he sent an email to all his friends saying, "And what did John Paul do for you on your birthday?!" That was just a few months before Pope John Paul died.

Flahaven, Mullaney and Hayden helped me a great deal. They were my mentors, and they introduced me to others, like Shannon. Jim had a quiet nature that was remarkable. He led our board retreat one year, and it was one of the best sessions we ever had. Jim was a gutsy guy, and I wish he had not held back so much in his book. Both Shannon and Flahavan wanted to be remembered as good soldiers, even though they had great differences with the church. Both were very spiritual, and both were loyal enough to the cause to want the church's blessing when they left the priesthood.

All of these heroes of mine were influenced by Pope John XXIII. When I interviewed with Flahavan in 1971, I asked him what kept him in the priesthood. I noted that most of his friends had left. His response was that the church kept him committed because it was such an effective platform for social justice. As long as he could be involved in effective social justice causes, he would stick with the priesthood. He went on to add, "Besides, what else would I do?" I said to myself, "My God, this guy is so politically savvy, he could be governor."

I remember having a beer with Dave Hogga, a classmate of mine at North Carolina who served two terms on the St. Paul City Council. I was telling him about the politics of the church. He was dealing with tough city issues and wild politicians. His comment was, "The problems of making city government work are nothing compared to trying to work one's way through the Catholic Church bureaucracy!"

The more I think about people who shaped my thinking and values, the more I realize how fortunate I have been. I have been at this job for 35 years, and I still love it. The thing that gives me the greatest satisfaction is building this organization. It requires a lot of people with different skills and talents who have to operate in a very challenging environment. When I started, I wanted people around me just like me. Now I know that building a large non-profit business requires people that are very diverse in terms of their ethnic background, intellectual skills and personalities.

One of the challenges of running an organization like Common Bond is that you want part of the business to be entrepreneurial and very creative, but other parts, like property management, have to be run carefully, with the same attentiveness and consistency day in and day out. It's like dairy farming: You got to be there at least twice a day! The development side and the resident services part of the business have to be creative and adaptable. So you are mixing people together with different skill sets.

My early career in architecture and city planning was very helpful to me. It is still important today, as we get into planning much larger and more complex multi-use projects. So my work is a blend of planning and design, mixed with entrepreneurial deal-making, topped off with the art of learning how to select, manage and motivate a very diverse organization. It is so satisfying to build something that you know can last. My personal growth has been extraordinary. If I had known 35 ago what I know today, we would have been dangerous! I wouldn't trade this experience for any other, even one that might have paid more money, or put me in a retirement community with all the so-called amenities.

As to the future, my biggest concern is what kind of people will lead these important organizations and communities 10, 15 or 30 years from now. A consultant told me a few years ago that our average age at Common Bond was 46. I thought that was great. She said, on the contrary, unless you start hiring only people in their 20s, that average age will keep rising! We have to figure out a way to build the capacity of the leaders of tomorrow in our key civic organizations. The urban leaders of tomorrow must have all of the basic business skills, along with sensitivity to social and ethnic diversity. It is not clear that we have the mechanisms in place yet to deliver these new leaders.

I enjoyed having someone like Peter Bell, an African American Republican and chair of the Metropolitan Council, on my board. We disagreed on many political, social and economic issues. However, the dialogue that took place on key issues, given his background and experience, was stimulating and productive. Many issues require extensive dialogue and debate if sound policies are going to evolve, and if each of the key players are to feel that they have been heard and own a piece of the ultimate decision.

What we do has to make sense to liberals, conservatives, middle of the roaders, people of all faiths, and maybe most importantly, young people. One of our greatest challenges is finding and developing the individuals who will be our future leaders during times of accelerating change and increased diversity.

As I think about what's needed from the next generation, I think about how proud I am of our kids and the support system they have had. John, the guy who kept me from being blown out of the sky in Vietnam, is now happily married and working as a developer of affordable housing, of all things! He's actually making money since he works for a very solid and innovative for-profit company, Metro Plains, based in St. Paul. Our daughter Kimberly is also an out-of-the-box thinker. She spent some time in the Peace Corps in Panama, continues her interest in natural healing and is developing her practice as a personal life coach. Kimberly's son, Nico, was born in Columbia, and is so creative he makes my head spin. Georgiann continues to be supportive to everyone in all of this, and like my mother, the spunk shows when the going gets tough. I can't help but be optimistic about the future with a supporting cast like this one!

SANDRA
L. VARGAS

T *he big issue for all of us is to determine what*
  kind of investments we should make now to raise
people out of poverty, keep kids in school, and prepare
our youth for the workforce of tomorrow.

– Sandra Vargas, June 2005.

I visited Sandra Vargas in her executive office at the Hennepin
County Government Center in June 2005. It was much like having a chat with an old family friend, which, by the way, she is.
There was little indication in the warmth and genuineness of her
demeanor that she bore the enormous responsibility of managing the operational affairs of Minnesota's largest county. When
she commented on her work, it related to the future, and new
or expanded programs to provide housing for the homeless, job
training for the unemployed, and better, more cost-effective service for all residents. Her own experience helps her relate to families in need and understand the important role that family plays
in building and maintaining healthy communities.

Perhaps the same drive that propelled her grandparents to
come north to an unfamiliar land made her multiple careers so
successful. Her business skills, ability to convert doubtful male
colleagues into respectful advocates, and mix of empathy and

hard-headedness, reflect an understanding of what propels people to do their very best. The other theme that has emerged during her remarkable career is the commitment to lifelong education. She has gone back to school many times during her professional career, while still playing the role of mother and wise elder to her large extended family. One leaves her office with a clear sense that one person can change the world, and that life is an incredible gift -- so work hard, help your neighbor, honor your family, and be joyful.

Since we met that day in 2005, Sandra Vargas has become the president of the Minneapolis Foundation, giving her an even broader platform from which to promote cultural advancement, social change and the kind of economic development that lifts Minnesotans out of poverty and promotes self-sufficiency. Sandra commented that she has more than three hundred relatives living in the Twin Cities area, all related to grandparents who originally came from Mexico. It is with them that she began her story.

My grandmothers and grandfathers were all born in Mexico, and crossed over with their families as children. My maternal grandparents were both very poor growing up in Texas, where they met as teenagers. Eventually they got married, and my mother was born in Texas.

As a couple, they had an entrepreneurial spirit and ran a little store. In 1924, they decided there was a better future going north through the migrant stream, and they brought my mother to work in the fields with their sisters and brothers. Mexican Americans were not being treated very well in the fields, which led my grandparents to settle in Minneapolis in 1925.

We were the typical Catholic Latino family at the time, with the pope encouraging large families. My grandparents lived on Lyndale Avenue North, so my mother grew up here and went to Minneapolis North High School. My grandmother was such an important influence in my life. She taught me certain values: take care of yourself, because you have to take care of your family, and remember that you are responsible to your family. She never sat down and stated these things directly. It was what I absorbed from the way she lived.

My mom and dad had eight children, in two groups. They had three right away. I was the oldest of those three, and then 12 years later my brother Ron was born, and then they had four additional children. As the oldest sibling, I was the parental child, and my youngest brother often seemed like my own child. I could relate to all of my siblings' aspirations and felt a sense of responsibility for their development. The women in my family were very strong. They were the ones who would gather and make the tough decisions – but would do so quietly, so as not to offend the men. Many of the women in my family were very powerful in terms of setting direction for their families and ensuring that life for their children was going to be better than it had been for them.

In the 1950s, my family moved to the suburbs. We had lived in close proximity to relatives before we moved to the suburbs, and after we moved, we didn't have a lot of interaction with our neighbors. Our "neighborhood" was still our family, with all the uncles, aunts and cousins gathering quite often. That extended family and the strong roles that both my mother and grandmother played had a tremendous influence on me.

My mother always had a vision for education. We were middle class, but probably in the very lowest rung, and we all went to Catholic schools. My mother had graduated from high school, but my dad had to work to support his family. He had also been a migrant worker. He had about a fourth grade education when he moved to Minnesota after the war. My dad was articulate, smart, quiet, and had good math skills. Together they made a very strong team, raising eight kids! I don't know how they managed that large a family. We first lived in Crystal, and then moved to a nice house in New Hope. My dad had been shot five times in World War II, leaving him partially disabled. His condition became worse as he grew older. He left the workforce earlier than most people—probably in his late 40s or early 50s. My mother went back to school in her mid-40s. She aspired to become a nurse, so she went to vocational school and got her LPN license just after their last child was born. She would put the baby to bed and then get out her books to study for her degree.

My parents went on vacation every September. One of my strongest memories is from when I was about eighteen, and was working full time. My grandmother would come to take care of the little kids during the day, and after work I would go home and take on the role of second mother. On the weekends I would usually clean the house, take care of the kids, and then hire a babysitter so I could go out on a date. That was an interesting role for me to play at that age. The concept of family responsibility was deeply ingrained in me—and I was learning first-hand about management to boot.

When I was very young, I didn't do well in school, perhaps because I thought I was different from other kids. By fourth grade, I began to excel, and continued through eighth grade in Catholic school, and then went to St. Margaret's. There was an eighth grade teacher that had a strong influence on me. She saw potential in me that I had never seen. I can remember early on trying to figure out what I wanted to be. I thought of things like working for a dry cleaner. There was no information coming to me about what the possibilities were. And my parents, as much as they wanted a better future for me, didn't have that information, either.

Late in high school, I met with a counselor and told her I wanted to be a doctor. She said, "Oh no, I think you want to be a nurse…it's more nurturing." You'd get that kind of response, even though my grades were good and my leadership skills were well known. My mother pushed me to do whatever I wanted. After high school graduation in the late 1960s, I visited relatives in Mexico City for a year, and went to the university there and learned Spanish. I dabbled in a lot of things in Mexico, but it was more of a fun year than one of serious study.

When I returned to Minnesota, my mother asked me what I was going to do. I told her that I might go to school, but needed a job first, so I went to work in a Honeywell factory for four years. Then some of my cousins decided to open a store in downtown Minneapolis. This was the family's entrepreneurial spirit surfacing. One of my cousins asked me to work for them. I told them I had no background for the job, but they believed I could do anything I set my mind to. I excelled in that job, and eventually became a store manager. That was probably the first glimpse I had of my own potential.

Later, I went to work for a man named Nolan Tanberg in Dinkytown. He was a terrific mentor for me. He taught me everything I needed to know about running a business. After several years of working for Nolan, I ran into Raphael Esparza from the state of Minnesota, and we decided to co-host a fashion show for Hispanic Month. Later, Raphael told me that the state was looking for someone in the Hispanic community with a business background – someone that could help with the "set aside" minority contracting program. The state wanted to do more business with the Hispanic community, and to that end, I was hired by the Department of Economic Development.

All of a sudden I found myself in a bureaucratic structure, without a job description and with only a vague charge of creating relationships with Hispanic businesses. I surveyed some of these leading businesses and talked about how state funding could help them. These visits evolved into the statewide Hispanic Chamber of Commerce, one of the first in the country. We held a large kick-off event with lots of Hispanic participation, and you could sense the entrepreneurialism running through the entire conference. The Hispanic Chamber of Commerce is thriving to this day.

Indeed it is. The Hispanic Chamber of Commerce of Minnesota continues to provide training, technical assistance, workforce development and other resources to Latino individuals and entrepreneurs. There are about 200,000 people of Hispanic/Latino heritage that make Minnesota their home, and the number is increasing rapidly. They comprise the largest ethnic group in Minnesota.

The word spread that the Department of Economic Development was going to downsize, so I applied for a job with the city of Minneapolis. At the time, I had been elected the first president of the Hispanic Chamber of Commerce. The job with the city involved the construction trades and minority business development. Apparently, the federal urban transit authority had told the city of Minneapolis that they could not receive a grant for transit operations unless they had a strong minority business development program.

At that time, it was not easy for some members of the African American community to see a Hispanic woman in the leadership role. It was a classic struggle of survival within minority communities. People like Ron Edwards, a Minneapolis African American civil rights activist, didn't think that I was the best person for the job. He would talk to city council member Walt Dziedzic, and together they would give me a hard time. On one occasion this evolved into a public hearing, where the press was supposed to show up and I was to be grilled. The night before the hearing, I asked my devoutly Catholic mother and grandmother to say a prayer for me. Sure enough, the next day there was an incredible snowstorm and the entire city was shut down. Who am I to doubt the power of prayer?! Fortunately, in lieu of a public hearing, we worked through our relationship and it got a little better, but those were the days when minority segments of the community operated out of a deficit mentality, making it hard to build the kind of relationships you need for positive change.

Several themes emerge as Sandra describes her progress in breaking down historic racial and ethnic stereotypes. First is the courage to take on extremely tough challenges. Perhaps this is rooted in her sense of responsibility to her family and culture. She understands what it means to others for her to be among the first to break new ground. The faith that springs from her Catholic upbringing is also a source of her strength. Next is a commitment to lifelong learning. She has the humility to realize that she doesn't know it all yet, despite her success. She also has the gift of a passionate need to explore the unknown. Finally, she has the innate social skill to open doors that lead to either advancement in her current job or greater opportunity in another field of endeavor.

As time went on, I got along famously with the African American community, but it took effort on both sides. What I tried to bring to that job for women and all minority businesses was extremely professional work, and an entrée into the construction trades through the city of Minneapolis. The job required very late nights, because during the day, I was under fire with all the politics involved. It was not an easy job, but I loved it. We had tremendous participation by women and minority-owned businesses during my three years there. I believe it was while I was at the city that people started to have confidence in me and my ability to put together programs that were fair and just for all contactors, regardless of ethnicity.

Then a job opened up at MnDOT—director of the Women and Minority Business Enterprise Program. Everyone advised me not to go there, saying MnDOT [Minnesota Department of Transportation] contractors are the hardest ones to deal with. That job turned out to be one of the best work experiences of my life. Within a large bureaucratic system—with a new regulation that says you must add minority contracting to the overall program—I learned that creating relationships with people is the most critical factor for success. When I first arrived at MnDOT and went to meetings with the Association of General Contractors, I would give a short speech to explain the new program. After one of these events a contractor came up to me and said, "I really like you, but I hate the type of work that you are doing." So they accepted me, but not the elements of the job I was doing.

The staff I put together was very multicultural, including Latinos and African Americans of both sexes. One day my supervisor asked how we got so much done with such a small staff. I think it was because my management style was highly participatory, allowing the team to bond well and have a clear vision and set of goals.

I also put together a small working group to figure out what was keeping small businesses from really getting into the construction industry. One of the key problems we found was access to working capital. We submitted a proposal to the Northwest Area Foundation and received a grant to establish a small working capital fund. The concept was that we would work through a bank that would make a working capital loan against a public contract, and we would guarantee up to 80 percent of the loan and provide technical assistance to the contractor. The contracts we supported involved trucking, demolition, construction, and landscaping, all related to highway construction. Some of the companies we worked with operated on a shoestring. Some of them are now sizable enough to compete with Mortenson and other large operations. That was very satisfying, especially since some of those contracts were so pivotal and significant in terms of creating wealth for people of color, including the American Indian community.

I had two mentors who helped me a lot. As a woman and an extrovert, I had moved into a male-dominated engineering environment that was quite introverted. In most cases, I was bringing bad news to people, in the sense that they had to change their way of doing business. My boss, assistant commissioner Larry McNamara, was just outstanding. He rose to the top of the organization from a basic labor job, and he understood what it was like to be an outsider and come into an organization of this size. Another manager, Bill Yoerg, made sure I sat on the management committee with fifteen senior engineers.

While I was working at MnDOT, I heard about St. Catherine's and decided to go to college on the weekends to get my bachelor of arts degree. It took me about four-and-a-half years of working all week and going to school on the weekends to get my degree. My major was business, with minors in economics and women's studies. It was all relevant because everything I was studying, I could take back to the office and try to apply. They used to kid me at the office and say, "Now she's on a marketing kick, so she must be studying marketing!"

When I started school at St Catherine's, I was married for the second time. I was in my late thirties and considering having children, although that never happened. After I graduated in 1991, the marriage fell apart. This is the area of our lives that I and many other women have struggled with. It sort of becomes an "either/or" option—either you can be really focused on your career, or you can make your personal and family life work. At least that's how it was at the time. There may have been an element of the traditional male Hispanic gender role in my relationship, too. While at some point I wanted to have my own children, there had also been that period when I raised my siblings as if they were my own. All of me had been poured into that role, and it was now behind me.

Ron McKinley of The Minneapolis Foundation recommended me for training at The Development and Training Institute. This was a fledgling national organization that was identifying social entrepreneurs and trying to bring them together to build skills. It really helped me think creatively about how to build businesses in low-income communities. At the time I was working with minority businesses, as well as heading the Hispanic Women's Development Corporation. We were trying to build a business with food carts that Latino women could buy into with sweat equity. It was an idea ahead of its time, and we could not get the funding. Later, of course, we saw these carts all over the place.

That experience produced other Latino leaders who have become very successful. For example, Lupe Serrano is the executive director of St. Paul-based Casa de Esperanza, and she is doing great work nationally and internationally around the issue of domestic violence prevention. Her message is that men and women have to work together to end domestic violence. Patti Tototzintle, the associate director of Casa de Esperanza, has done consulting work for the Wilder Foundation and is also a very strong leader in the community. Recently the two of them researched the new Latino immigrants in Minnesota. They conducted 160 interviews, and learned that many, if not most, undocumented immigrants do not speak English. Casa de Esperanza set up three computers in Mercado Central, located in Minneapolis at Bloomington Avenue and Lake

Street, and also provides fully bilingual services for immigrants. Casa de Esperanza and Hennepin County are now examining ways to partner in order to provide new immigrants with a boost, so that they can become self-sufficient. I have remained very close to Lupe and Patti, since we shared that training experience twenty years ago. Incidentally, I have been on the Development and Training Institute's Board for the past several years, and was recently elected chairperson of the Board.

Another experience that helped me become a more effective leader was attending HISPANA, the National Hispanic Women's Leadership Program. I participated in 1992, while I was still with MnDOT. At the first HISPANA meeting, in California, I met the twenty-eight women in my class. We had to write about where we wanted to be in five years, as well as a paragraph on exactly what kind of work we wanted to do. I remember writing that I wanted to be chairperson of the Metropolitan Council. I'm so relieved I did not get that role! However, the moment I wrote it down, it generated energy for me, and I knew I wanted to eventually manage some large system. The second meeting of HISPANA was at Harvard, at the Kennedy School of Government. It was at this point that I decided I wanted to attend Harvard, so several years later I applied for a Bush Leadership Fellowship and went to the Kennedy School to earn a master of public administration degree. It was amazing to me that I could take a leave of absence from MnDOT, and overnight leave the world of work and become a student again. I also took several classes at the Harvard Business School and was interested to learn that they also offer classes on social entrepreneurialism. Harvard was a place that allowed me to make a number of excellent new connections. I graduated in 1996, when I was in my late forties.

When I went to Harvard, my two brothers moved into my home in south Minneapolis and took care of everything—including my cat and dog—allowing me to totally immerse myself in this new experience. It was wonderful. My apartment at Harvard was a gathering point for my extended family. There were times when there were nine relatives staying with me in my two-bedroom, two-bathroom apartment! My five-year-old niece, Sierra, came to visit, and said she felt there was something special about me. When she returned home and got back to kindergarten, she told her teacher that she had been to Harvard! She is now fifteen and still has a goal of attending the Kennedy School of Government! She is a straight-A student, plays the cello, dances, and is a strong leader. At the time, I never thought that simple exposure—just a visit during her kindergarten year—could be a transforming experience for a child.

Without being fully aware of it, I had evolved into the head of our large extended family. My grandmother had predicted this might happen, and had told me so years earlier—although I did not fully comprehend what she was saying at the time. The role of leader is not always one that a person seeks; sometimes it just creeps up on you over time, based on your actions in life. My youngest sister is very entrepreneurial, and it's very likely that she is the one who will evolve as the next head of our extremely large extended family. My nieces are all very responsible, too, and will be strong leaders in the future. Both women and men in my family played an enormous role in my life. I just happened to be the person in the family with leadership vision.

After I graduated from Harvard, I went back to MnDOT. At that point, it seemed the engineers only could see another engineer as the leader of the organization. I knew that my career growth would be limited, so I started looking for another job. Nearly fourteen months later, in November 1997, I was hired as deputy administrator for Hennepin County. Kathy O'Brien was the Minneapolis City Coordinator at the time, and a helpful mentor for me. For the first fourteen months, I worked under Jeff Spartz. Then the CEO of Hennepin County Medical Center, John Bloomberg, took another job and Jeff decided to apply for that vacated position. At first, I didn't position myself to take the job of county administrator. Someone asked me if I wanted the job, and I said something like, "I guess so." That person responded, "Well, then you better get going!" I was hired as acting county administrator in February

1999, and given the official title of Hennepin County administrator in June 1999. Hennepin County is a huge organization with a nearly $2 billion budget. The county is responsible for criminal justice, human services, public works—including all the county roads—the twenty-six suburban libraries, the garbage burner and alternative sources of energy.

While at the county, I was especially proud of working to end generational poverty. But when I left the county in March 2007, we had yet to figure out a way to move families into higher economic strata. We focused on decentralizing the work and partnering more closely with the non-profit community to develop more successful approaches. I still want to create an environment in Minneapolis and Minnesota that is more based on the assets of a community. Fred LeFleur is heading a study that tracks twenty-five families struggling with generational poverty. There are many opportunities for new approaches and new applications of information technology systems. With limited budgets likely to continue well into the future, our communities are being forced to innovate. This is compelling us to get at the root causes of social problems, dealing with issues at the front end of the process rather than always dealing with problems after they occur. Throughout my tenure at Hennepin County, I always believed that taxpayers were exactly right in demanding better results for the investment they made in government.

There is still a lot of exciting work to be done. The challenge of working with diverse groups and watching the people we serve improve their lives is very uplifting. The relatively new work with diversity training around the county is most heartening. Some municipalities used to resist this, but now they see it as a necessity. The big issue for all of us is to determine what kind of investments we should make now to raise people out of poverty, keep kids in school, and prepare our youth for the workforce of tomorrow. Sometimes the short-term problems threaten to overwhelm us, but it is essential to stay focused on the future and take calculated risks to ensure a higher quality of life for everyone in the years to come.

RICHARD ERICSON

*M**any of the good rehabilitative programs in our prisons are being cut back. We are back to warehousing prisoners. The leadership and statesmanship just aren't there like they once were. Hopefully the cycle will turn, when the cost of not effectively investing in our future catches up with us.*

– Richard Ericson, April 2004

Dick Ericson had been retired for five years from the Council on Crime and Justice when we met at his home in the northeast suburbs of the Twin Cities in April 2004. There was a youthful enthusiasm to Dick that belied his 71 years. His focus in retirement was his family. He laughed as he described how his grandson by his first marriage referred to Dick's young son by a much-later second marriage as "unc."

For 32 years, Dick employed that same warmth and energy for the betterment of Minnesota's criminal justice system. He was president of the Council on Crime and Justice, an organization formed in 1957 as the Prisoners Aid Society to help rehabilitate prisoners, improve correctional policies and practices, educate the public, conduct correctional system research, and encourage crime prevention. In recent years, its mission has been broadened to include the victim as well as the offender. In large part because of the Council's efforts, the Minnesota corrections system has been considered a national model of efficiency, fairness and effectiveness in safeguarding the public.

Corrections is a field many volunteers shy away from. Dick changed that in Minnesota. He had a genius for innovation and salesmanship that attracted many civic leaders and business executives to the cause of insuring that Minnesota's criminal justice system performs at its highest potential. He brought together the best and brightest from government, labor, business, the foundation community and other concerned civic organizations. As a result, what was once a struggling community-based non-profit, responding to a few basic needs in the criminal justice system, became one of the premier agencies of its kind in the United States. His impact was not just local, but national. If there were a *Social Entrepreneurs Hall of Fame*, Dick would be in it. Dick Ericson and the Citizens Council were clearly in the forefront of the professionalism required to reduce the rate of recidivism in our prisons so that men and women can return to the workforce despite a previous run-in with the law.

The emphasis Dick gave in our conversation to his early years illustrates his deep appreciation for family and neighborhood. His story begins on the North Side of Chicago.

My mom's name was Sonia, but everybody called her "Sunny." She was outgoing, full of life, and at her best when people were around. I remember her taking in people, often someone new to the neighborhood who needed a place to live. My dad was not the instigator of these outreach efforts, but he went along with my mom's charitable spirit. He had a great sense of humor and enjoyed gabbing with visitors, as long as they talked loud. He had a hearing problem.

I grew up with my mother's mother in the house, Grandma Margaret Carlson. We called her "Maska." She came over in 1893 from Sweden, on the same boat with King [then Prince] Gustav V.

She came as a beauty queen, showing up at various events at the 1893 Chicago World's Fair. She stayed in Chicago when the other girls in her party went back to Sweden. She lived with us until she was killed by a streetcar on Clark Street when I was in the sixth grade. There was a bunch of old Swedes around, and we always had a lot of people around coming over for dinner and conversation.

Despite some strong racism in the neighborhood, Mom had people of color over. I always thought my parents were very accepting of people, regardless of their race or if they were completely new to the neighborhood. I don't think my mom's attitude was contrived, or part of any established philosophy. It just came naturally to her because it was the right thing to do.

She was the product of an immigrant family who was welcomed to America. Her father died when she was twelve, and her mother, my grandmother, cleaned houses. My mother left school and went to work after eighth grade. She could type like a whiz, and was a secretary for many years.

My parents had no great formal education. My father quit school in the eighth grade. They were poor, but generous. I remember the church bringing us food baskets when my dad went on strike at International Harvester. It was an interesting time. We of course had one car. Nobody had two cars in the neighborhood. We always had to rent, and never owned our home. I never cut a lawn until I was an adult. I remember asking my neighbor when we moved to St. Louis Park, "Do you cut the lawn clockwise or counterclockwise?" But life was good, and we never felt deprived. We could walk to Lake Michigan and fish or swim by jumping off the rocks. We had ball parks close by. All of us kids went to the same school, played basketball and baseball together, and had a great time. It was a great neighborhood. My younger brother and I had a lot of buddies.

I was born in 1933, during the Depression. My dad had been laid off as a tool and die maker. He and his father decided they would buy a farm and provide food for the rest of our extended family. My father had five brothers, and their families were large. I was raised the first three years on a farm near Mora, Minnesota. We had no running water or electricity, but we were able to send potatoes and vegetables back to Chicago. Finally my mother said, "That's enough," and we moved back to Chicago, where she could push her babies on Clark Street. By 1936, the economy was improving.

Much later, when my parents retired, they moved to Spectacle Lake near Cambridge, Minnesota, and rented a house from me that I built with my dad's help. It got hit one day by lightning, and the fire department came. Where was my mother but out in the kitchen, making coffee and putting cookies out for the firefighters?! This was just typical of my mother.

My dad's parents also came on a boat from Sweden around the turn of the century. My grandfather on my dad's side was kind of gruff and aloof. He was an intimidating person. My dad liked to talk about them having the first car in the neighborhood. They were a little better off than many because my grandfather was an engineer, good with mechanical things. This rubbed off on my dad. He could fix just about anything.

Hard work was a given in Ericson's youth, but so was his father's example of striving to get a job right the first time. He learned early the carpenter's maxim, "Measure twice, and cut once." This story reveals much about the father's impression on the son:

In 1974, I had an old Ford Ferguson tractor at our lake home near Cambridge. Pa and I decided to build a log splitter that would run off the tractor. So we accumulated iron pieces in Minneapolis, and with a little help from a welder, we put together a log splitter that was supposed to run off the power take-off of this tractor. I can remember standing up on the tractor and wondering if it would work, since there had been no testing as we built it. There were no detailed plans; we just put it together as we went along. I was up top, and Pa was watching to see if the wedge would move forward on the splitter. When the wedge moved forward I really got excited and yelled, "Pa, Pa, it works!" I still remember his crisp two word answer: "It should've!"

I often think about that story in the context of those other, harder times. When you build things, they are supposed to work. You couldn't afford to think about what might go wrong. My dad's times required optimism and tremendous self-confidence, at least at the level of mechanical things. Where you couldn't afford to hire repair work done and had to do it all yourself, tackling new thing brings with it an almost naive self-confidence. Of course you will succeed. You must.

That kind of rubbed off on me. There is no perfect transference of these lessons to my later career, but I think when you learn to do things on your own, you are not afraid to step out to pick up new challenges. My father never went beyond his mechanical background, nor did he invest or take much risk. He was a product of the Depression years, when simply surviving was a great victory. But my situation was different. As events turned out, risk-taking almost became a habit with me.

Dick described growing up in a close-knit, working-class Swedish-American community, where home and church combined to impart traditional values.

As kids, we didn't speak up much at night around the dining room table. You were to eat and get on with your homework. My parents protected us a lot from the violence of the world beyond. They took Life magazine, but didn't let us read about the gory parts of World War II. There was conversation about the war at dinner because about 70 percent of the younger men at church and in the neighborhood had been drafted. All over the neighborhood, there were the little flags in the windows. Blue stars depicted those serving in the war, and gold stars were for those who had been killed. We pulled wagons around picking up paper for the war effort.

This was a very tight neighborhood, with the homes close together. In addition to our Swedish and Baptist friends, there were

Catholics and Jews. We had friends among all those groups, even though there were considerable feelings among the adults that we might be tainted because of these relationships. "Lake Wobegon" attitudes are very familiar to me.

Sunday was a huge deal at the church. We would go to a prayer meeting early to pray for the day, then Sunday school, and then church. As we got older, we would sing at the prisons at noon, and then we would have a young people's service, followed by evening service after which we had "Singspiration." We young teenagers would go out on Lake Michigan and sing and do our best to put our arms around the girls! Our parents didn't know about the latter. Church was the social deal. Our parent's didn't like us to go to non-church parties. They were afraid we might be necking and getting into trouble. What they didn't know was that we were doing the same thing with God's blessing!

This was a group of very conservative folks who never spent much time talking about personal or philosophical issues. They were focused on their daily work, getting the kids off to school and putting food on the table. The people of my parents' generation had to deal with very heavy day-to-day challenges, and so their world in many ways was very small. This was of necessity. Their outside world basically revolved around the church and its activities. But they were a part of one of the most generous groups you could possibly imagine. This was all at a time when people were losing their jobs, but they still went out to visit the sick and reach out to one another. If someone couldn't shop, you went shopping for them. You would not think of not helping someone who was in trouble. Problems got solved in the neighborhood, and church was the key to the social relationships and making the neighborhood work.

In grade school, I skipped a grade. There were fifty-three kids in the sixth grade and only forty-eight desks. So they chose somebody to skip to the seventh grade. This was about 1944. I was not originally picked to skip, but a girl named Harriet came back after lunch and told the teacher that her parents would not let her skip. So the next day the teacher came over and said, "Ericson, you're moving ahead a grade." I came home for lunch and told my mother that I just moved a grade forward, and my mother never questioned the teacher's judgment. I was then one of the youngest kids in the seventh grade. Those were fun years. I had a paper route, and was also a school patrolman on the corner near our apartment.

I was not always one of the best-behaved kids in school. Even in high school, I would get a lot of check marks on my report card indicating that I didn't sit still enough to please the teacher. My friends and I would occasionally skip school and just hang out. I graduated in the last quarter of my class, and almost didn't graduate. There was one day when my father had to get me back into school after being suspended. Later, he made me pay him for the half day of work he missed! I did well in shop class and in the course in architectural drawing. In fact, I won a competition citywide for designing and building a model house. I always scored high in spatial relations activities and tests, but I didn't pay much attention in other areas. My vision was to grow up and become a carpenter. Most everybody I knew in my age group was a tradesman. College was not part of the culture. The day after I graduated from high school, at age seventeen, I was on the roof of a house serving as an apprentice carpenter, getting blisters on my hands. The old Swede carpenters wondered if I was tough enough.

I served as an apprentice carpenter for about three years, and lived at home. I worked for a man named Gus Gustafson with a heavy Swedish accent, and his son-in-law Harry Lindberg. I loved the work, and I was always building something and helping out somewhere. I thoroughly enjoyed the people, and even volunteered to help remodel our church. Some of us goofed off once in a while, but as time went on, I developed a real solid work ethic. You did, or you were fired.

Then I volunteered for the draft. I did basic training at Fort Leonard Wood, then served one year in Germany at the end of the Korean War. While in the Army, I realized that the people digging the holes had no college degree, while most of the men supervising, telling you where to dig, had some higher education. I was invited to go to Officer's Candidate School, but that would have meant another nine months. Actually, I did so well on the tests that they sent me to Fort Belvoir to a rock-crushing school. Can you imagine that?! I was in the combat engineers, learning to build roads and bridges.

I got married while in the Army. I had met my first wife Carol earlier, and she came by plane to Germany. We traveled all over the place, skied in Garmisch, visited Munich, and had a wonderful time. One weekend we went to Paris by bus for $13.50! We had met when I was nineteen, on an evangelical trip across the country. We thought we would save the world.

Dick came home to Chicago determined to try college and a career that did not involve blisters on his hands. His decision wasn't cheered by his family, for whom college represented another world. His father counseled: "Richard, I hope you don't change your mind about anything."

After the Army, I started at Wright Junior College for one year, and then on to Roosevelt University for the last two years, and got my B.A. I did it in three years because I was in a hurry. As a veteran, I did not have to take certain classes. Our children, Lynn and David, were born when I was about twenty-three or so. I was going to school and working as a carpenter part time. So it was school in the morning, carpentry in the afternoon and then school again at night. This could never have happened without the G.I. Bill. I majored in sociology and minored in psychology. Roosevelt University is a downtown college with a no-frills campus. It was convenient. I could take the subway and get their fast and cheap. We were still living on the North Side, at Foster and Damen. I was a Cubs fan and went to Bears games. We had a lot of fun with church league baseball on summer evenings.

I was accepted at the University of Chicago in the Graduate School of Social Service Administration. Before starting the grad program, I helped my parents build their first home. My dad had retired, and I had told him, "Pa, when you retire, I will help you build a house." So we talked them into buying a lot in Sawyer, Michigan, a two-hour ride from Chicago. My dad and I built a house. We dug the foundation, framed it, put the windows in and sided it, all in six weeks. He subsequently finished it off with occasional weekend help from me. After that, I went to graduate school for two years, and majored in corrections as a field within the graduate program. I came out of the University of Chicago with a master's degree in 1961, and worked as a federal parole agent.

My interest in helping troubled people goes back to a man I met through our church when I was in high school, Harry Lindberg. He was the co-owner of the Gustafson & Lindberg construction firm where I'd earned my journeyman's certificate. He got me to volunteer at Sunny Ridge Family Center in Wheaton, Illinois, where I worked with a lot of kids that were in trouble. I had grown up in a somewhat similar environment, and could identify with those kids. The idea that these kids were to be discarded was not part of my thinking.

That was the beginning of my interest in rehabilitation and helping kids that were in trouble. I was intrigued by the mystery of what made these kids the way they were. The question, "How it is that people commit crimes?' still fascinates me. That behavior is so goofy. Over the years, I have found many of these people to be very interesting and engaging. They are complex, but absolutely fascinating. What causes their behavior, how you deal with it and prevent it, fascinated me. That early exposure and my own intellectual curiosity pushed me in the direction of corrections as a career.

As a federal parole agent in my last year in graduate school, I had a caseload of people who had committed crimes on military reservations, or had crossed state lines in the course of committing various crimes. I had read a book by a Minnesotan, Paul Keve, called *The Probation Officer Investigates*. He was the head of Hennepin County Court Services, which worked with kids and adults on probation. So after graduate school, I applied for a job with Keve as a juvenile probation officer in Hennepin County. He hired me at $5,280 a year in 1961. That was like gold. We were in clover. We drove up to Minnesota with two little kids, Lynn and David, pulling a U-Haul, and bought a house in St. Louis Park for $17,300.

Looking back, I really needed to get away from Chicago. I had drifted away from the culture of being a carpenter, though to this day I love carpentry and woodworking as an avocation. I needed to identify myself as a corrections professional. My identity had been that of an apprentice boy for Gunderson & Lindberg. I was also moving away from the fundamentalist theology of my former church. The literal interpretation of the Bible no longer worked for me. My thinking with respect to human rights and issues of equality didn't sell well in my old culture. When the job with Hennepin County came about, Carol and I were both ready to move on.

I was first assigned to work in the Richfield area. Next, I was promoted to assistant superintendent of the Hennepin County Juvenile Detention Center. I continued in that position for a while, then worked three years at the Minneapolis Rehabilitation Center, working with parolees from the prison in St. Cloud, Minnesota. I was again recruited by Paul Keve to work at Correctional Service of Minnesota, a private, not-for-profit outfit. Paul was chair of its board of directors.

I had also been teaching part time at Bethel College in St. Paul. Carol was at the University of Minnesota, where she earned her B.A., M.A. and Ph.D. in the College of Education. We lived in St. Louis Park, where the kids went to school, and subsequently moved to Arden Hills, where I built our home on weekends. Building my own house gave me a break from my work, where it is often difficult day to day to measure one's contribution. When you frame your own home, you can see the results! I always had a need to design something and then see it work.

When I ran a parolee rehab program for the Minneapolis Rehabilitation Center, I worked for a man named Bob Will. It was a federally-funded program working with parolees out of the St. Cloud Reformatory to see if there were better ways to integrate them back into the community. It had a sophisticated research component. We set up a control group and measured the effectiveness of our program against parolees who had not benefited from our work. It gave me a certain amount of confidence when I saw that our clients were outperforming the control group. It showed that the right combination of positive and negative incentives can make a difference. People do have the capacity for change.

This was important to my future work. I was there about a year when a St. Paul business executive named Reuel Harmon and the board of directors offered me the presidency of the Minnesota Council on Crime and Justice. That was 1967, and I started at $11,000 with a staff of two. The annual budget was $47,000. Reuel Harmon was chairman of the board for several years, and was a strong advocate for the best criminal justice system practices.

The organization had been founded in 1957 by Allan Hubanks and the American Association of University Women, the latter encouraged by Helen Rustin. Helen had been involved in a study commission set up by then-Governor Luther Youngdahl to determine why people were failing on parole and winding up back in prison. The recommendation was that there should be more services to help parolees reenter the system. Ben Berger, a businessman whose ventures included the Minneapolis Lakers, was the financial angel, and also instrumental in getting the organization going. Correctional Service of Minnesota, the predecessor to The Council, was launched. Its mission was very broad—to look at ways to improve the criminal justice system from the cop on the beat to the court room, to the prison system and the re-entry back into society.

We had a terrific board of directors and staff through all of the thirty-two years I was president. Our offices were on First Avenue North in Minneapolis, where the Target Center now stands. Reuel Harmon was very helpful in those days, particularly through his closeness to then-Governor Harold LeVander. We got LeVander to agree to a number of progressive criminal justice system practices. That taught me how important it was to have the right people on one's team to influence key political decisions. There had been two organizations running in parallel, The Citizens Council and Correctional Services of Minnesota. One was a study and research group, and the other did the civil and legal services. I decided to merge the two and brought the two boards together after I couldn't figure out which letterhead to use!

We expanded the board with Bill Sweasy, CEO of Red Wing Shoes, Leonard Murray, CEO of Soo Line Railroad, Julian Baird, chairman of First National Bank, and other CEOs. Helen Rustin of Minneapolis was the spiritual conscience of the board, encouraging us not to shy away from politically tough issues. Chuck Dietz from 3M came on, as did David Haskin, at the time with Dayton's. It was a high-powered board. I was able to hire some highly-skilled people like Russ Stricker, who is still working to protect the community with creative programs for offender rehabilitation.

By the time I retired, we employed 115 people and had a budget of $4.5 million. We were operating in 1999 at 11 different sites. I made my share of mistakes, and then some, running the place, but it was always interesting and fun. We moved several times over the years. We moved to the "seven corners" area of Minneapolis shortly after I started, where we took over a building that had been a flop house. We were the host agency for HIRED at that location. HIRED has now grown to serve over 8,000 individuals annually with employment and training services. We didn't always succeed in helping individuals, but we were stubborn in our efforts to try.

One of my favorite cases was that of Art Dilworth, who was in and out of prison many times. He had imagination and creativity but just couldn't stop stealing. When I taught my first criminology class, I asked Art to join me. He was the only black person in an all-white class, and his job was to "steal" a purse from someone in the class and then beat it out of the room. So at a break, he grabs a purse and takes off and hides. After the break, a young woman came back and said, "Where is my purse?" I said, "I don't know, what happened?" She said, "Well, where is the guy who was sitting here?" I told them I would look around, and came back in with Art saying I had nabbed this guy. By this time, many were realizing this was a set-up. I used this episode as a way of asking the students what we should do about this guy who had committed this offense. We'd talk about proportionality in sentencing, racism, his past criminal history and a host of other issues. Art was one of the great cons of the world. He eventually got grey hair and, I believe, straightened out. In any case, he was one of the real-life offenders, along with a host of other criminal justice system practitioners, that I enjoyed bringing to the classroom during the sixteen years I taught criminal justice courses part-time.

Art Dilworth became well known at the bank where I worked, Northwestern National Bank of Minneapolis. He arrived at my desk one morning after visiting with the president of the bank. He told the president that he had been doing business with the bank for several years. As I learned later, the business he had done—check forgery—landed him in prison. The president, John Moorhead, got a big laugh out of that. Art had met my wife, Anne, at a non-profit organization benefit and learned that I worked at the bank. He talked me into going on the board of HIRE (later renamed HIRED) which helped ex-offenders retrain and find work. It turned out to be a great learning experience for me. In his criminally active days, Art devised various schemes of passing bad checks, including disappearing ink and ink with a delayed action acid that literally ate up the check after it was cashed. He had a host of other schemes that were a tribute to his creativity, but not his integrity. I became a mentor to Art, but unfortunately, his criminally-inclined creative juices landed him behind bars again. Eventually, he aged and tired of his schemes. What was remarkable to me was his ability to fantasize the most incredible schemes. It was a source of great humor for him to relay his exploits and contemplate even greater schemes. I am unaware that he ever harmed anyone physically. His drive was pure con-artist creativity.

Dick could engage people ranging from Art Dilworth to corporate CEOs in the council's work. He was able to attract influential men and women to the field by challenging them intellectually, and pointing out the cost-effectiveness of a highly professional criminal justice system. His ingenuity and enthusiasm were infectious. He could also effectively make an audience see that "there but for the grace of God go I."

There I was, leading this agency, running around getting grants, teaching, hiring staff, and generally having a great time. I loved innovation and taking new approaches to tough issues. It was relatively easy to get folks involved because the field was intriguing to people who were inclined to volunteer. The mystery of offenders, cops, and prisons, and how it all worked, was fascinating to people. Civic leaders wondered how we could fix this terrible social issue of community crime. We pulled together many study groups. I was amazed at the degree of interest in these issues by so many different segments of the community, including business and the professions. The tough part was raising money. It's not easy to feel sympathetic to criminals when so many other social issues like homelessness, poverty, and physical disability are more appealing to the philanthropic community. However, when I asked people to serve, they generally were very supportive. I always tried to anticipate what the next area of interest might be with respect to the entire criminal justice field. "Where would there be a chance for innovation and positive change?" was the question that directed my thinking.

That thinking led in 1976 to a program to assist victims of crime. Russ Stricker led the research that got us a three-year commitment of $150,000 from the Northwest Area Foundation to start a program offering emergency services for victims. It was a matching grant; they gave us the first $50,000, and if the Legislature would match that for the first year, the remaining $100,000 would be funded. That allowed us to pull in all kinds of people to help educate their legislators. Eventually we received the funding to start a series of crime victim centers. This was in 1977 or thereabouts, when Leonard Murray of the Soo Line Railroad was board chair. Gov. Rudy Perpich became interested in the victim movement.

Republican civic leaders were extremely helpful. They helped me gain an audience with legislators. As we built the board and gained more business leaders, they in turn were able to leverage their relationships with others to help us build our financial base. There is this Minnesota thing with business leaders. They call on each other on behalf of their favorite charity. It's a form of deal making that they find fun, and it's great for the community.

Dick paid tribute to the wide range of community leaders that supported his work. They included corporate officers, including many CEOs, elected officials, foundation executives and civic leaders from prominent families of all ethic backgrounds. They comprise a full generation of this state's community activists. Among them: Mrs. Duane Andreas, David J. Winton, David's brother Charlie Winton, Martha Atwater, Harold Bonnell, Rudy Boschwitz, Gladys Brooks, Ellis Bullock, Virginia Meyers, Bill Hammock, Phil Harder, Evelyn Gosco, Geri Joseph, Oscar Howard, Mike Winton, Anne Heegaard, Tom Beckley, Jim Hetland, Bill Sweasy, David Nasby, Bob Provost, David Haskin, Chuck Dietz and Ken Krupf.

The talent Ericson attracted and the research his efforts funded translated into credibility and leadership for the Council on state corrections policy. As a result, Minnesota's thinking about how to respond to crime changed.

We became an important voice for a rational, fair, and effective criminal justice system, and spoke out against the accepted wisdom that increasing prison time is the only way to reduce crime in our communities. Because of our research and quality programming, we were a useful source for the news media when they asked questions about proposals in the criminal justice system. At the Legislature, we became a credible source of politically impartial information, with bipartisan support from key community leaders. In fact at one legislative hearing, when a new high-security prison was recommended for juvenile offenders, the author of the bill stood up and said, "Well if the Citizens Council is going to oppose this, I'm not going to carry the bill." That is the kind of credibility we worked for. We were able to get a foster family bill through the Legislature. This helped reduce the overcrowded conditions at Red Wing [the state's juvenile detention facility.]

The juvenile code at that time provided that you could become a juvenile delinquent if you were a danger to yourself. We researched this issue, and convinced a legislator from Chaska that this made no sense, and was harmful to both the juveniles and the taxpayers. We got this clause removed from the code. There was also a bill advocated by the former St. Paul police chief that provided that each individual crime would have a specific determinant sentence attached to it, with no range permitted. This was a departure from historic judicial practice. We opposed this, though we supported guidelines, and lost in committee. When it went to the floor of the House, every constituency wanted its own specific sentence for a particular crime, be it auto theft or stealing a cow. There were thirty-two amendments of this type, and it passed the Senate. When it got to Governor Wendell Anderson's desk, his chief of staff, Tom Kelm, asked, "Is there a problem with this bill?" I said yes, and explained the technical reasons why the bill should not be signed. He persuaded the governor to veto it.

In the next session, we along with others recommended the establishment of a formal Sentencing Guidelines Commission. With the help of House Republicans Arne Carlson (the future governor) and Gary Flakne, who was the committee chair for this matter, Minnesota got the Sentencing Guidelines Commission established. This was a remarkable accomplishment at that time. This was also about the time when, with the help of Gov. Perpich, the state put up major funding for crime victims centers, which the agency still runs thirty years later.

Much of our work was behind the scenes on policy matters, so we were able to offer advice to both Republicans and Democrats without getting the credit, but also without getting branded as conservative or liberal "bleeding hearts." However, when one senator referred to me as "Chief Bleeding Heart," I was honored. We helped design the new prison at Oak Park Heights. The politics of prison location is a hot issue with many legislators who, for example, wanted to convert an out-of-date mental health facility in Faribault or Moose Lake into a prison to support the local economy.

We started a program called WOW, "Women Outside the Walls." This was a program aimed at supporting the families of inmates and therefore making rehabilitation efforts for inmates more effective. In that same vein, we started a parenting program for inmates in the prisons, which was helpful to the children and the inmate.

We later developed a program called "victim-offender mediation," and I hired a professional named Mark Umbreit, an early pioneer in this field. I also hired Kay Pranis for that program. She is now the most knowledgeable and most respected person in the country on victim-offender "circles" programs. The idea is to bring offenders and victims together to help the victim, and also to help the criminal realize the pain he or she had caused. After being scoffed at initially, the program has gained wide acceptance and has expanded across the country. Our own program grew and attracted funding from individuals and foundations, including the United Way. This program was a unique way to hold offenders accountable, get damage repaired, and have the community involved in the decision about consequences.

Prior to this program, criminal justice was an abstract idea. The notion was that the offender would "pay back the state" for the damage caused. The idea was that the state should get "its pound of flesh out of the offender." With the victim-offender mediation program, the victim actually gets some repair of the damage incurred, in terms of mental and emotional satisfaction. The offender in many cases realizes he has to say "I'm sorry," and often that has positive results. It was surprising to me at first how tough little macho delinquents would swagger into a room, but before they were over apologizing and realizing the emotional damage they had caused by theft of personal items, they would sometimes be in tears. The whole idea made a lot of sense economically; it brought the offender in touch with the consequences of his act; it offered the victim some relief, and it provided the state with a new and effective program of consequence with rehab potential. It also helped the community to better understand some of the underlining causes of juvenile crime such as poverty, racism, disruptive home environment, and lack of proper medical care. Mark Umbreit and Kay Pranis really were significant in putting put this whole concept on the map for the entire country. The Council can rightly feel proud of its role in bringing these ideas to the field.

These are illustrations of what can happen when you have a clever staff and an able board, willing to take some risk. Not every grant worked out well. We had a $60,000 grant from The Bush Foundation for a program on criminal justice education that didn't work. I told Humphrey Doermann, then the Bush Foundation president, that the program simply didn't work as we had hoped. He later told me how important that statement was because they learned what didn't work, and also because they knew we could be trusted to tell the truth. They gave us many more grants over the years. We also received numerous grants from scores of other foundations. The key was innovation, risk taking, and integrity.

In the late 1980s, I was getting a little bored and run down, and programs were getting harder to fund. It was getting harder to be creative. I even applied for a job to run the 3M Foundation. Fortunately, an insider got the job. Instead we embarked on a new exciting venture. The idea of owning income-producing real estate while solving our own office needs got me re-energized. I went to Jim Shannon at the General Mills Foundation and asked him for $50,000 to do a tax study. My question was, can a non-profit 501(C)3 be the general partner in a limited partnership? We got the grant, did the study and the answer came back: Yes.

I then went to my friend Howard Rekstad, who was familiar with selling limited partnerships. I asked him if he could sell thirty-five people at $20,000 apiece, and he did it! The advantage to them was three-fold: first, potential equity buildup; second, tax-advantaged investment (this was prior to 1986) and finally, merging these interests with their social service goals. The next move was to get David Haskin on our board to have his company guarantee $250,000 of debt. The Bush Foundation gave us $125,000. Chuck Dietz of 3M got his company to guarantee $250,000. First Bank through Jim Hetland gave us a $400,000 loan to buy a 40,000-square-foot warehouse on Third Street. Tom Beckley of the Soo Line was board chair and supported the project. We spent $2.5 million to rehab the building, and moved in 1986. We rented two floors to Hennepin County for programs run by Mike Weber, and eventually our rental income rose to $260,000 per year. We later bought out the limited partners, had a capital fund drive to pay down the debt, and wound up with valuable space and a steady source of cash flow.

Had we not made many good friends over the years who knew us and respected our work, we never could have raised the kind of money needed to buy the building and pay down a large portion of the debt. We were one of a few limited partnerships that had deals like this that paid off its limited partners in full, and with a 6 percent interest rate.

After putting in thirty-two years at the Council, I don't remember one day when I wasn't excited about going to work, even though I was exhausted at times. I had a great career. When I left, we were working with twenty thousand people, had a great staff and a superb board of directors. Sure, there were some slow periods, and financing the operation was a challenge right to the end, but it was a great experience. There are days when I would like to get back into the fray, as I see some of our state's progressive policies we worked so hard at slip away. My wife Becky, who is an economist and evaluates programs, and I are saddened by what we see as bad decision-making on the part the legislature, especially in the area of sentencing. For example, the legislature can't resist messing around in what should be the province of the Sentencing Guidelines Commission. Many good rehabilitative programs in our prisons are being cut back. We are back to warehousing prisoners.

The leadership and statesmanship just aren't there like they once were. Hopefully the cycle will turn, when the cost of not effectively investing in our future catches up with us. The true operating costs of incarceration are running at about $40,000 per inmate per year. When you add overhead to that, like central office administration, the true cost exceeds $50,000 per individual. This doesn't even include the construction and building maintenance expenses. So the cost to the public is going up as rehabilitation programs are cut. These extended sentences for people doing drugs are really taking up the space that should be reserved for hardened criminals doing rape and murder. Many studies, to say nothing of common sense, show that in the case of less severe crimes, a three-year sentence with good programming generally has better results than a ten-year sentence under the warehousing approach. Of course, punishment has its place, but prevention should be the focus of where we invest our resources.

How shocked we were to learn on August 10, 2006 that Dick Ericson had died suddenly from a heart attack. His health had been excellent. Dick was a very close personal friend who spent many evenings at our home. We miss him like a lost brother. Memories of his caring nature, hearty laughter and wise counsel remain with us. Tom Johnson, the former Hennepin County attorney who succeeded Dick at the Council on Crime and Justice, said of Dick: "Dick was a person of tremendous energy, creativity and compassion. As a result of his work, the Council developed its reputation for innovation and balance. Dick's many achievements include the Minnesota Corrections Act, advancement of victims rights, the founding of the Center for Reducing Rural Violence and development of restorative justice as a respected philosophical framework in the United States. To meet Dick was to remember him. Let us remember him today for his many contributions to a more just society."

JOHN DURAND

*A*t the end, we had demonstrated that we could employ over 1,300 individuals and generate $58 million in commercial revenues annually with more that 62 percent of the employees having a severe disability. That is what I did, but just as important was the love I felt for so many individuals whom God kept putting in my way.

– John Durand, April 2002

I find it remarkable that a single individual, sensing both a need and opportunity, can provide the magic that allows a social enterprise to flourish. To be sure, serendipity also plays a role. Had John Durand not been introduced to Sister Anna Marie, Minnesota Diversified Industries likely would never have existed. But even more remarkable was John's acceptance of a job that paid 50 percent less than other job offers he was considering. This was not an easy decision for a young couple just starting out. Clearly, John was ready, both intellectually and emotionally, when the call came.

John built Minnesota Diversified Industries into a large nonprofit organization that provides employment at competitive wages for people with a range of physical, emotional, and mental challenges. MDI has provided training and employment for over 1,000 individuals annually in a business setting that nurtures self-sufficiency, productivity, and social interaction. MDI offers disabled people every opportunity to recognize and work toward their full potential.

Building and managing a successful non-profit is tough enough. Add to those imperatives the need for the sensitivity and know-how to train people with severe disabilities, and you have an enormous challenge—one that is not likely to be met without a deep love of people. Perhaps that is what John gave back from a caring mother, father and adoring step-grandmother. His family was close and supportive during economic times so tough that neighbors were required to share if they were to survive. A key to John's successful career, I believe, is the wide range of family, work, and social interactions he experienced growing up.

There was no need for me to record John's story. He had already written a memoir entitled, "I've Been Growing Up My Whole Life." It was originally written exclusively for his family; I am grateful that he allowed me to excerpt from it. The memoir is a remarkable accomplishment, and should inspire each of us to write our own stories. While details that would be of interest to only the family have been excluded, key elements of the story, including the evolution of MDI, remain in John's own words.

I was born December 10, 1934, in St. Paul, into a family that was led by my grandfather. A family war had been triggered by a challenge to the way he believed life should be lived. My grandfather was unable to accept a non-Catholic as the person my father would live with for the rest of his life. My parents were married, even though it caused a break in the family that could have been irreconcilable.

When I was born, my mother and father had already started their family with the birth of my sister Donna Jean in July 1933. Donna was the eleventh generation of our family to be born in North America and the third to be born in the United States.

The person I knew as my grandmother was Ella Clark, who was not my father's mother but my grandfather's second wife. My grandfather would go on to outlive three wives, and his third wife Mary was more than twenty years younger than him, and died years before him. I can think of no one I would have rather had for a grandmother and godmother than Ella Clark. She must have had a really difficult life, to be willing to take responsibility for my grandfather's nine living children and her own son. She was always warm and affectionate with me, and made me believe that there was nothing I could not tell her, even if it was just about my feelings. She was the mother I needed, because my own mother was too busy caring for the next of her ten children.

During the summer, Ella would invite me to their house for extended stays of two or more weeks, to help put in the garden and paint the white picket fence around their entire yard. We had secrets that were just ours. She found a secret hiding place where my lead soldiers and my bank (a Prince Albert tobacco can) were hidden from all the other grandchildren. It was really wonderful for me, because I had her all to myself without having to share her with anyone. Every day was more special then the day before.

When my grandmother died, I made an extremely serious mistake that I would live with for more than fifty years. I was thirteen years old, and the grief hurt so much that I made a promise to myself that I would never love anyone that much again. I believed it could not be good to love and need someone that much. I did not cry at her funeral because my father would not have approved of my crying. He would perceive it as unmanly of me. When my father died fifty years later, I cried, and that was because I finally had been brave enough to love someone again so much that crying was the only way to express what I was feeling.

The economy had not recovered from the 1929 stock market crash when I was born, and my father found work as a carpenter at the new Wards store at 25 cents an hour. That meant that for a 40-hour week, he would earn $10. With that, we lived better than most newly-created families, because we had our own apartment.

My grandfather DuRand could not help financially, as he did later with loans, because he had lost everything but his house on Cathedral Hill in the stock market crash. During this period, our family never thought we were poor, even though it must have been very difficult for my parents.

My parents rented a second-floor conversion of a house at 429 Sherburne in Frogtown. Frogtown got its name from all the French people who lived there, because the non-French said we sounded like a frog croaking when we would talk. My mother and father rented the second-floor conversion even though it had not been finished. They rarely saw things as they were, but envisioned what they could become. In 1938 my parents bought their first home at 1674 Rice Street in St. Paul, in the Highland Park neighborhood, next to the house my grandfather DuRand built.

I remember the night my dad took Mom, Donna, Darryl (Skip), Scott and me to see that house. The electricity had been turned off. We stopped at the store and got a box of farmer's matches, and while he carried Scott, he lit matches so my mother could see the home they would buy the next day. The house was built on a double lot, and had three bedrooms, one for my sister, one for my parents and one for us three boys. Skip, Scott and I would share a bedroom for the next thirteen years and be as close as any brothers could be, even though we had our disagreements and fights at times. When we were five and almost seven, we were given our first set of boxing gloves by my dad's brother Leo, and quickly learned how to settle disputes when words could not.

After my sister Barbara was born, it was seven years before the next five children were born. We first five children would always see ourselves as the first of two families. Those of us who were the big five believed we were unique, and knew our experiences with the world could not be replicated by the younger five. This was a most wonderful time of my life, when I believed that everything would go on forever, and only things chosen by me would change.

A lot of what we did and gave up during that time was about the war effort. We saved our tin cans, cooking fat, newspapers, old aluminum cookware, and our tires, all of which were placed in front of the house on the curb on a given day. Meat, sugar, butter, coffee, gas, and tires were rationed. The worst of all was we had to give up our dad, who went to work in Kentucky as a civilian in the war effort. That was something that cost me fifty years of what could have been an intimate relationship with him. That relationship was not recovered until our last ten years together.

My father taught me how to see myself in a world that was full of individuals with purpose and value. My parents had purchased a set of encyclopedias, *The Book of Knowledge*, and I would spend night after night on the living room floor searching for facts and information that would be useful to me. One night while searching, I found a page where there was a picture of a hammer and saw along with some ordinary tools that were well known to me. I said, "Why would they put these things in here, when everybody knows what they are?" My father did not miss the opportunity, and quickly asked me, "What is a shaft level?" I had to say, "I don't know." He then said each of us has knowledge that others might not have, but this does not elevate us or put others down.

My mother demonstrated how special each of us was to her by planning a special day for each of us to be alone with her. This would be in addition to when she would take all five of us on a riverboat cruise down the Mississippi River on an old stern wheeler, or to the State Fair in the fall just before school would start. She would sometimes hold our hand in a way that let us know how much she loved us, and how very proud she was to be our mother.

My school days started at age four, earlier than most. I asked so many questions in my attempt to understand the world, and would be so persistent with my pursuit of why, where, and how everything fit into our world, that my mother came to recognize she needed help with me. Help was available under a special admittance policy that the St. Paul school system had. Any child could be tested at age four, and with enough score, would be admitted to school that year rather than waiting for the mandatory age of five. I scored high enough that while I attended St. James, my second school, the nuns told my mother that I had the highest IQ in the school. My mother was very kind and never shared that fact with me until I was out of the service, nor did she ever use it to challenge my sometimes less-than-stellar performance in high school.

My first day at school, my mom walked me to Riverside School, just the two of us, and that made me feel special. When my mom entered the classroom with me and said, "This is my son," I could feel pride and love in what she was saying. Then it was time for her to let go of my hand and allow someone else to enter my life.

It was at a summer school that two wonderful things happened to me. The first was that I met my first black person. Until then I had lived in a totally white world and would only see black people in movies or magazines, never having the opportunity to know that they were just like me. The second was that our teacher demonstrated to me that I could write, even though I couldn't spell. The rule was that our story would be graded on everything but spelling. I wrote a wonderful story because for the first time I could use the word that belonged there, rather than the one I thought I could spell. At the same time my academic skills were developing, there was the necessity to develop the required social skills to survive as the smallest kid in the class. That didn't take a lot of thought. Just remember four basic rules: it was good not to be too visible; not to be seen as a possible challenge to the kids who ran the place; as the smallest in your class, you were not going to lead on the playground; and finally, be satisfied with classroom performance. It really took some kids a long time to learn those simple rules. In junior high, I added a few new ones: your wit and humor could prevent unnecessary pain; alliances were stronger than an expanded perception of one's self, and placing yourself closer to where others saw you made really good sense.

At Sibley Junior High, I learned how to come back from the dead. One day my eighth grade English teacher, Miss Bundy, confronted me in the library for not doing what I was assigned. My response to her was not one of my better moves. Her response was quick, and I found her hand square on my face. With her being my English teacher and my passing in some doubt, what I had done was downright stupid. If I were to fail English, it would mean I would not be a candidate for acceptance to Cretin High School. The next day she presented me with a lifetime opportunity. In class, she announced that she was directing a group of students that would perform a marionette show for the elementary students, and asked those who were interested to let her know. She was the most surprised person in the world when I asked to join her troupe, and quickly accepted. There turned out to be just one boy and eight girls, and the boy was me. I worked really hard on that performance as the captain of the guard, and won her praise and a passing grade, even with my inability to spell. This was truly being resurrected from the dead.

I was accepted into Cretin, which was a prep school run by the Christian Brothers and the U.S. Army as a junior ROTC program. When I started Cretin, we lived at 150 West Wentworth in Dakota County, and the closest transportation was the end of the Hamline Cherokee streetcar line, two miles from our house. The walk in the spring and fall was just fine; in the winter, it was horrible. The conductor or motorman on the street car was called Frenchie, and the two of us became special friends. Being late for school would earn you demerits, and for that reason, I was always there for his 7 a.m. run. He would save Indian head pennies for me, and I would help shovel coal into the bunker heaters under the street car that would heat the cars in the winter.

You would have to classify some of my experiences at Cretin as tough love. The brother we had for general science in our freshman year would give a test each Friday, and on Monday we would bend over a desk and receive a swat with his paddle for each point below seventy we had scored. I only had to lay across the desk for him once before giving science my highest priority for study on Thursday nights.

Some of my goals and objectives changed a number of times, but a few were fixed. I believed that contacts made at Cretin would serve me well for the rest of my life; my training would be excellent preparation for serving in the armed forces; and that I should accept a challenge, and finish what others had not or would not do. I graduated from Cretin in 1952, and at the same time completed my first successful career, in the hotel industry.

Knowing how to work is the most undervalued skill we humans use, or misuse. It is not taught in school. If our parents don't know how, they can't teach us how to work. I asked more of our 1,300-plus employees to leave our company because they didn't know how to work than for any other reason. We would always work with anyone to teach a specific skill that we needed if he or she knew how to work, but MDI lacked the time and resources to teach non-disabled how to work. My parents taught me how to work, and that primary skill was the reason for my being as successful as I was.

There was a period in about the fourth grade where a school friend asked me to help him take over his older brother's paper route. The first thing I learned was how to smoke like the other paper boys, while we rolled our paper at the drop-off corner. Helping him would eventually lead to my brother Skip and me getting our own paper route, and learning that every morning meant every morning, icy cold winter as well as beautiful summer mornings. My next paid work was on the truck farms in Dakota County, where we moved when I finished the sixth grade at St. Francis de Sales. Mr. Ramisch had a large-enough truck farm so that he could feed and care for a family of four just from the income the farm generated. He would pay us three cents a bushel for pulling, topping and bagging onions, and ten cents a bushel to pick green beans.

My next paid employment began a week after we moved from Wentworth to Robert Street in St. Paul. This was at Mack's grocery store. While I worked for Mack, Barney Husneik heard about me from one of his employees, and because he needed someone to take care of his produce section and wash the floor after the store closed, I became his target. He offered me forty cents an hour, almost twice as much as Mac was paying me. I presented Barney with the idea of freezing corn on the cob during the season and then selling the corn later when it was not available. We had to call the University of Minnesota to find out how to process sweet corn for freezing.

Someone told me that the Hotel St. Paul was paying seventy-five cents an hour for dishwashers. I went to apply, even though I was not sixteen, the required age. With me being in a uniform, they would only ask to see my Social Security card, which did not have my age or date of birth on it. I was immediately hired and told to start work the next day. I worked as a dishwasher after school and on weekends. One day, the chef asked me to see him in his office. He told me to go to the linen room and get a steward's coat, because I was his new kitchen steward for nights and weekends. I was responsible for the dishwashers in the main kitchen, the coffee shop, and the grill, as well as the food runners and the janitors who hauled the garbage and did the floors. After graduation, the hotel business manager asked me if I would work the front desk at night. Not long after starting as night clerk, the hotel manager asked to see me and said that they would like to send me to New York to hotel management school. That forced me to admit that I had lied about my age when starting work at the hotel, and to share with them my plans to join the Air Force as soon as I was eighteen.

Graduation from Cretin meant that I could begin my career in the military. Arriving at the courthouse, I prepared myself for the worst, even though I really believed that I had done quite well on the tests. An officer introduced himself, and said that he was with a new unit of military intelligence and wanted me to think about joining them in the Army Security Agency. By the time basic training was completed, my crypto clearance had been approved. I later found out that the FBI talked to almost everyone I ever knew, even going so far as to talk to the mother of a girl that I had only dated twice.

While in Korea, I had four meritorious promotions in sixty-five days and was made responsible for eighty-seven Koreans and Chinese civilians. I served with the 501ST Group north of Seoul.

Before I left Korea, the ASA gave me four choices: Africa, Turkey, Philippine Islands, or Two Rock Ranch Station in California to choose for my next duty station. By this time I had found out that wars just don't kill and maim combatants. Children and old people are killed indiscriminately. I did not want to have any more to do with military life.

John left the Army, and returned to Minnesota to work for his father, who headed a carpentry business that also involved his grandfather. He was restless, but he enjoyed the people he met, especially a certain waitress.

Ardyce and I met when we were both working at North Town Center in Lexington, Minnesota, on the same day in 1958. She was filling in for a friend who was sick at the restaurant, and I was building a bowling alley in the same center. I had arrived at my usual time to start work at 6 a.m. and wanted to have breakfast. I asked for two poached eggs and dark toast. She told me they were out of poached eggs. I later found that she did not know how to make poached eggs. I found it very funny when she said they had fried or scrambled, and asked, which would I prefer? After some small talk and growing interest on my part, I asked if she would like to go dancing with me the next Saturday night. She said yes, and we arranged to meet at her house on Sunset Road at 7:30 p.m.

After we were dating for two months, it became apparent that my feelings for her were very deep. One night I got down on my hands and knees in my motel room asking God for help in being able to live the rest of my life with Ardyce. One of my friends worked for a jeweler, and I went to see him and bought a diamond ring. Then I went to her house and found Ardyce vacuuming her room in her slip. I sat on the bed and proposed. When I asked her to marry me, Ardyce looked troubled, but said yes even though she was only eighteen. I was twenty-five by then. She was very mature for her age. Later I would find out that the troubled look was because she was not sure if she wanted to marry anyone that early in her life.

Our first apartment was in what was referred to as Little Italy in northeast Minneapolis, where Italian was spoken in the store, bar, and one mass every Sunday at our church. We lived in a converted second floor at 618 Buchanan Street. We chose the location because it was clean and less than two miles from Honeywell, where Ardyce worked for the next eleven years. She worked in the security department, where she was responsible for all classified documents. She was also responsible for arranging clearances for all employees who would visit government installations any where in the United States.

We were blessed with two wonderful children, Jacques and Monique, who have enriched our lives immensely. When I would become aware of someone's love for me, a new courage was born that would let me believe that everything in the universe was possible.

My brother Skip and I started Triangle Construction Company, doing both home and commercial renovations. We were as compatible as any two partners could ever be on a job site. We were profitable right from the start, and never doubted our future success. One day on the way home from a job, I turned on the car radio and heard President John Kennedy make his famous speech, "Ask not what your country can do for you; ask what you can do for your country." The next morning, before Ardyce and I had each left for work, I said that I really would like to go back to school. That day a financial plan developed while I was at work, and it was very difficult to wait to get home to share it with Ardyce. I would receive the GI Bill for three more years. Additional money would be earned by working summers as a carpenter, and building custom millwork and furniture in the garage/cabinet shop we built in our backyard.

When they accepted me at the University of Minnesota, it was for General College, not the Institute of Technology that I had applied for. After making the Dean's List the first and second quarter, they allowed me to begin taking classes in IT and pursue my goal of becoming an electrical engineer. Science was my love. Then one day Howard Nelson, the chair of the department of Industrial

Education, invited me to join his department, and said if I did, he would graduate me before my GI Bill ran out. He was a man of his word. He had a plan for me that he did not share until the last quarter, when job interviewing began at college and commercial firms. When Howard saw that my interviews were getting serious, he called me in and said, "Please go to this interview as a favor to me, and ask for Anna Marie and inform her that Howard sent you."

When I arrived at the address on Summit Avenue across from St. Thomas College, the sign "Christ Child School for Exceptional Children" had me really confused. After waiting in the reception area for a few minutes, I was shown in to see Anna Marie. Well it wasn't Anna Marie, but Sister Anna Marie in her wheel chair, just as she was twenty years before, when my parents sent me to her to learn how to spell. Among the children she was teaching at the Christ Child were students who were mentally disabled and were not being served by the archdiocese's elementary education programs. Their parents joined together and asked Sister if she would please help educate their children. Her response was to create Christ Child School for Exceptional Children.

After the two of us caught up on what had happened to each of us over the past twenty years, she asked me to push her wheelchair while we visited her classrooms. While we were touring, she kept saying, "It is such a shame that all this work by these dedicated teachers will have no purpose, since when they graduate they only go home and watch TV for the rest of their lives." When we returned to her office, she asked me to give her just three years of my life so that we could create new outcomes for her disabled students. At that point, I really felt an external force take over, and without thinking about the consequences, I agreed. God sometimes directs our lives when we let go and listen with our heart.

Saying yes to her was easy. But how would I ever tell Ardyce that I had just agreed to a contract at less than half a commercial offer, and a lot less then what my earnings were before returning to school? That evening when she was told, her response was without

194

delay: "You surely are at the right place, a school for the mentally disabled! You will fit right in!" Graduation came, and I graduated with honors. Ardyce said she was proud of what I had accomplished. The statement should have been what we had accomplished. It would have been nice for the two of us to take a vacation to wind down, but it was necessary for us to go to work right away. I would go back to work as a carpenter, and Ardyce as the assistant to the director of security. We would need to earn enough to carry us through that first year contract with Sister Anna Marie.

The first day on my new job, I walked up to the Zimmerman home where a new adventure would begin. Sister Cedille, whom I had not yet met, was at the door and said, "I see you are wearing pants. Well, act like it when you work with her!" She meant Sister Anna Marie. She knew what she was talking about. It wasn't long before we were all calling Sister Anna Marie "Sam" when she wasn't there. She was as tough and directed as anyone I'd ever encountered. However, it has been said that I was no pushover either. Sam and I worked very hard at a common goal and kept personalities out of the mix for three-and-a-half years. She was a leader, and her being a woman was immaterial. She was able to share her vision of "all graduates being prepared to become gainfully employed after graduation" from the extension school we would create. Her vision was to recreate the high school industrial arts programs for the boys and home economics for the girls. She was convinced that mentally disabled students were being unnecessarily excluded from mainstream education.

Here was a new school building with all new equipment, and teachers who were being paid by an endowment fund. How did it happen? Sister and her friends did pray, but after they prayed, she went to a luncheon that was honoring her work at The Christ Child Center. She was at the head table with Richard Lilly, president of the First National Bank of St. Paul. He had just experienced a near fatal car accident on the High Bridge in St. Paul on his way home from work. After hearing her story of how she was recovering from her own accident and what she had done in spite of her own disabilities, he was really impressed. After lunch, he reached over and, while patting her arm, said, "If there is anything that I can do, please let me know."

That same week she wrote him a letter telling how wonderful it would be if she had a school of her own, and that there was a house on Summit Avenue for sale that would be just fine. R.C. Lilly bought the house and paid for the renovation. The next year, she informed him she had run out of room and needed more space. R.C. then purchased the house next door and tore them both down to build a new school with classrooms, therapy suites, offices, a gym and caretaker residences. R.C. Lilly would go on to establish an endowment for the school before his death.

The next week, I was introduced to our new boss, Bishop James P. Shannon, who was also the president of St. Thomas College just across the street. Bishop Shannon was very supportive of our efforts, and kept us out of sight from the archbishop, who was closing schools and making other cuts due to financial shortfalls. Jim Shannon would reenter my life more than ten years later, after he left the Catholic Church over its birth control position. He helped me while he was at the Minneapolis Foundation, and later at the General Mills Foundation. Jim Shannon became one of the strongest supporters I have ever had, and a dear friend.

Never having a class in special education in school left me with a lot of concern about my students that first day. I could not differentiate between mental retardation and mental illness. There were seven boys that first day in the first session and six in the second session. They were all believed to be in the educable range, after Sister retested them all. Although she was not certified to do such testing, she needed to prove a point with their parents. When she challenged the parents to spend more time with their children doing homework, they said there was little reason to do that, when the children had been found to be not educable by their local school. Sister told the parents that their schools had made a mistake, and she was going to prove it by personally retesting them all! She would change the parent's actions by changing how they thought about their children.

Before long, I knew that the way to prepare disabled students for work was to have them work. Using indirect methods of instruction, such as an industrial arts program, wasn't as effective. Changing Sister's mind about this could best be done with a demonstration. Mike Shaffer, a student in the St. Thomas social work program, asked if he could do an internship with us. Mike was not only good but a hard worker, and soon he had our first contract from Random Specialties in Hopkins, Minnesota. They were receiving sewing needles in wooden crates from Japan. The needles were held in black paper sleeves in soldered tin cans. They needed to have the needle packages removed from their packing and placed in new boxes, all facing the same way. From that point the needles would be placed into little mending kits of the sort you receive in a hotel room. My method was to create a lot of specialists that would do just one small part of the job, just as my father had done on housing projects. The contract was a success, and Random became a regular customer of Christ Child Extension School.

We had now been certified to receive state funds for training disabled students from the St. Paul school system, thanks largely to a lot of work by Vern Shultz and Gene Stellman. But we needed a name change. Sam was against it at first, but when shown that our religious name was getting in the way of grants from foundations and government bodies, she agreed to the change. Our new name would be The Occupational Training Center or just OTC to everyone in the state of Minnesota.

Along with the new name, I initiated a new approach to obtaining funds. I resolved never to ask for operating funds from foundations or corporate giving programs. I would limit my request to startup funding and expansion funds, with a promise we would never be back to request ongoing operating funding.

Within the year, John Taylor, the director of the Northwest Area Foundation along with Paul Olson, introduced me to a new funding method. It was called PRI, or project related investment. It was a loan below normal bank interest rates, and with a repayment schedule designed in conjunction with a foundation. Such a loan would only meet your needs if you truly believed that what you were merchandising could be profitable. I never sold a foundation anything that I did not believe could be a success—but then my mother taught us we could do anything.

Mom would never let us use the word "can't." She would tell us over and over again, "There is nothing that you can't do. Sometimes it will be difficult, and at other times you may need help, but everything is possible." When she would ask us to do something that we thought to be very difficult, rather then say "we can't," we would have to say why we thought it would be difficult, and what we would need before we could do it. Sometimes we would need additional information, knowledge, experience, or the help of others. This way of thinking served me well for the rest of my life.

When OTC outgrew the storefront on Grand Avenue, the search for more room took us to Washington D.C. and a meeting with Dr. William Usdane at the Department of Health, Education and Welfare. To present our case in the best light, we needed a plan for an educational building that was nothing like those built before, and with the capacity to house experimental programs. With our concept plans, we went to D.C. and were awarded a grant almost on the spot. When the grant was made public, Sam said we would use another architect because the building looked like a radiator. When I explained that the outside could look any way she wanted, she still said no. I had to make a choice: go back on our word, or leave Christ Child Services Inc. and allow them to do what I knew to be unjust, but without me having anything to do with it. I chose the latter. After notifying the board of my decision, the archbishop sent Father Ray Lucker (himself a future bishop) to see me, and he asked if I would take over Christ Child Services. I said no. I could not be part of taking the school that she had built away from Sam. He then asked what would happen to the extension school if I left, and I said, "Why don't I take it with me and leave the elementary program for Sam?" He asked what I would need to do this, and I told him $100 to open a bank account. He asked Monsignor [Ambrose] Hayden to write the check, and the deal was done. That weekend, I put together a transition program that would not only affect the change in corporate structure, but also the rest of my life!

After calling all the staff together, I informed them that I would be leaving Christ Child Services and starting a new company, The Occupational Training Center Inc., outside of the present organization. Those who chose to be part of this new quest compiled an inventory of our assets and identified those that would be useful to the new venture. We had a small contract with Honeywell to modify some rammed iron castings that could be expanded, and continuing contracts with Random Specialties. We had an excellent working relationship with VR Services for the State of Minnesota and St. Paul Schools to serve some of their disabled students under a service agreement with the Special Education and Rehabilitation Department. What we did not have was a facility or operating funds. There was one place that satisfied our needs, and that was on University Avenue in the Midway area of St. Paul.

I went to see Howard Nelson, and the two of us wrote articles of incorporation for the Occupational Training Center. Howard agreed to serve on the first board, and said I should go meet Henry Tiechrow, the state director for manpower development. Tiech and I hit it off on our first meeting, since we had much in common in our backgrounds. He introduced me to Burghly Saunders, a manager of manpower training and development for Univac who was also the former superintendent of schools in St. Paul. I then met Jane Donnelly through Betty Hubbard, who was president of the St. Paul Association of Retarded Citizens and had become a fan of what we had been doing. Jane was a parent and a state lobbyist for the Minnesota Association of Retarded Citizens. Her husband was a partner with the Oppenheimer, Wolff and Donnelly law firm. Jane and her husband David would give immediate social visibility to our new OTC. With those four board members, we incorporated, with the help of David and his law firm at no cost to us. Moving from a storefront on Grand Avenue to a 14,000-square-foot building on University Avenue gave OTC immediate recognition. We could now be seen by the public in a new way.

The 1968 federal Vocational Education Amendments were responsible for stimulating efforts by vocational schools nationwide to begin serving special needs students. The federal government mandated that 25 percent of their education funds be spent on services for students with special needs. This happened very quickly, because the public schools were confronted with declining enrollment for the first time in thirty years and teachers were being laid off. This new legislation would be a distraction from my work at OTC, because Howard Nelson asked me to develop a graduate program to prepare administrators and educators to carry out and monitor these new educational programs and services being mandated by Congress. We taught the course together at the University of Minnesota for four years. At the same time Henry Tiechrow asked me to develop a training program for the state in vocational education.

It was at this time that we developed an alternative to vocational evaluation that was eventually adopted by facilities nationwide. My idea was, if you want to find out how someone will function in a particular trade area, place him in one, or a replica of one, and see. The observation should be done by someone who is competent in that specific area. It started in 1968 with developing offsite training (now called supported employment.) It was co-funded by special education, vocational rehabilitation, and vocational education. We created sites in the box-making industry, sewing industry, heavy equipment manufacturing, restaurant and cafeteria business, and nursing homes. Within our facility, we created a body shop, machine shop, welding shop, print shop, trade bindery, hospital room, and related academics programs. In addition to serving students from St. Paul and suburban schools, we were now serving those who were being released from state institutions.

A number of individuals who had been in training for a number of years were now becoming static. They were the ones whom we lacked the resources to move into the commercial or public sectors of employment. These same individuals were gainfully employed at OTC working on subcontracts from major corporations, but at a rate less than 25 percent of the industry standard. They still had student status, but were without funding from any state or local agency. There was no alternative available in our community other than to send them home, if we could not or did not create an alternative outcome. This is when we created "Midway Learning and Manufacturing" on Raymond Avenue, one block from OTC. We assigned those individuals whom we believed had demonstrated that they would not be ready for outside placement in employment within the next year to MLM, and a new status was created. They would now become clients, not students.

One day a mother arrived at OTC with a thirty-four-year-old son who had never been to school or any other program. His whole life had been lived at home. She asked me if I could do anything for her son John. I determined that John would be given a job as a packer, because his mistakes would not damage products during their fabrication process and could be dumped out and recounted if an error had occurred. We began that morning. I knew I would quickly have to have John counting to five. At noon, we had made no noticeable progress. After lunch we seemed to hit a wall. The next morning John and I started again, and at the 10 a.m. break, we had made no progress. In total frustration, I turned to Jane, one of the other packers who had a learning disability and said, "You teach him how to pack those damned things!" Jane said yes, turned to John, held up her hand with her five fingers spread and said, "Give me this many," and John did, by dragging one pack out with each of his five fingers just as Jane was doing. Who was the teacher?

Our goal of being financially viable became the cornerstone of our enterprise. We developed a track record of total repayment on each of our PRI or foundation loans. Our banking relationship improved overnight. It was Tom Hartzell, another self-made man, who went to the bank, unknown to me, and co-signed for a $100,000 line of credit. He was one of our champions until he was killed in a plane crash in Alaska. Another champion was John Carroll of American Hoist and Derrick of St. Paul. His reputation was that of a hard-nosed businessman. At our first meeting, John looked at me in a way only he could, that said "Don't blow smoke down my back and tell me my ass is on fire," and said, "What is it you are doing that has the interest of Tiech?" I told him that we wanted to provide those individuals who had been denied career training the most appropriate training we could. He then said, "Sign me up." John became a real mentor, and that included me being dressed down by him in front of the OTC board for a less-than-stellar performance on a property acquisition. John would always make excuses for not touring the facility, and one day when I was really pressing him, he told me why. He said, "John, I could not look at all those disabled individuals and keep it together."

After I returned from a stint in Canada designing the adult services segment of that country's new comprehensive service system in 1973, the U.S. Supreme Court handed down a ruling on disabled children and their education. The Court ruled that every child must be educated by public education, without regard to what or how severe their handicap or disability was. This meant that public education had a new mandate, and that it would create a new way of serving those with disabilities. We already knew that not everyone could be placed into commercial employment at the completion of mandatory education. Some individuals need post-school support to be gainfully employed. Our enterprise could become the first step in their career by serving as their employer.

We now needed a new facility. We were packed in so that we were losing efficiency and potential customers. Tom Hartzell told me of the Donaldson Building, just five blocks away. After arranging a tour of all 123,000 square feet of the facility, I told the owner that if he let us move in and lease it for $1,000 per month, I could save them the maintenance costs until I raised the funds to buy it. My three-year balloon was coming due on the University Avenue building, and I would need to sell it to pay off the owner of the new building. We found a buyer within two weeks, and Frank Donaldson approved our move into his building.

The federal government had just created the Office for Developmental Disabilities and established a regional office in Chicago, with Robert Vogt as director. I called Bob and asked for a meeting to discuss a new delivery system that I was sure would reduce government spending on employment of persons with severe career-related disabilities by 40 percent. It would at the same time serve those who had been rejected by Vocational Rehabilitation because they were thought to be too severely disabled to benefit from rehabilitation. I went on to say that in three years, I could decrease the need for government funding from 50 percent to 10 percent, a huge shift. Sheltered workshops at that time required anywhere from 50 percent to 70 percent of their funding from charitable and government sources, while serving a less disabled population than we had set out to serve. I would copy the ancient apprenticeship model, where each apprentice would work with a skilled journeyman and learn not only the skills of the trade but also the social protocols. The survival rate in the competitive world of employment is near zero when an individual lacks the required social protocols of a craft or trade.

Bob had the required funds to make things happen. To raise the required $100,000 of local matching funds, I called John Carroll. When I arrived at his office, he gave his wallet to his secretary and told her not to give it back to him until after I left! I said, "I won't ask you for any more if you tell me how to raise $100,000 and give us the chance to be independent." He got excited about the plan and sent me to see Ron Hubbs, the CEO of the St. Paul Companies. After telling Mr. Hubbs of my plan to create a commercial enterprise capable of providing employment for individuals who were severely disabled with little or no government funding, he began to smile. He quickly said, here is the first $25,000, and here is who you should go see to get the rest.

The door opened right away with Don Larson at 3M. He agreed

to match the $25,000 that the St. Paul Companies was contributing. The next call was to Paul Verette at the Saint Paul Foundation, and Paul's pledge made it $75,000. With only $25,000 to go, the last one to see was my best friend and president of Coca Cola Midwest, Bob Moore. He signed on with, "Here we go again, John changing the world," and I replied, "No, just how people think, and the world will change itself if we can recognize it."

We would operate under two names for three years, OTC and the new venture, Minnesota Diversified Industries, a name chosen by the management team I had selected from OTC. The management team was lead by Rick Twedwell and included Margaret Lowery, Pat Palmer and Gary Flesland. Margaret and Gary had been hired by me when I purchased Black Born Bindery from Dave Nicolson. This business would serve as the base of the new enterprise we had created. The employees of the enterprise did what was required and what they were all trained to do. In three years, they reduced their need for subsidy to 8 percent. We had exceeded our goal! However, at OTC, we were still involved in organizational welfare with the state of Minnesota. If any profit was made, the state would reduce our next year's allocation by the same amount and leave us with no funds to invest in new technology and automation. We restarted the entire enterprise as Minnesota Diversified Industries, a not-for-profit corporation dedicated to creating a profit and removing ourselves entirely from government welfare rolls.

Achieving that goal would mean some real belt-tightening, and that meant leaving behind some of our management and technical people. We would recreate ourselves and have a single unified corporate structure. My first task was to meet with our investors and share with them what we were going to do, and with their help, how we planned to get there. The first one on board was Ted Hamm, with a $47,000 gift to cover the next payroll until we could put in place permanent financing. The permanent financing came from a one-time loan guarantee of $1,000,000 by Jaye Dyer, CEO of Dyco Petroleum. Jaye was a real entrepreneur in every sense of the word, and was MDI's fearless champion. He helped me grow and become all that I was capable of with the God-given talents I had. Everyone should be fortunate enough to have such a friend.

There were days when all I thought I needed was ten minutes without a problem to solve. But what I really needed was a site manager for the St. Paul Pelham Avenue Plant. With daily issues cared for, I would be able to focus on developing an ongoing plan for growth and financial independence. Rick Twedwell recommended Ted Gilson for the job. Ted was the best promotion I have ever made. He would go on to serve as vice president of manufacturing and president of government services for more than thirty years.

To facilitate better communications with management, I developed a one-page management report that asked the following questions: 1) What are your objectives for the week, and what are their priority ranking? 2) What assistance from other managers will you need? 3) What additional manpower will you need? 4) What other resources will you need? 5) What opportunities do you see for MDI? 6) What did you accomplish last week? The report was given orally to the whole team and placed on file in my office so I could see what priority objectives were not getting addressed.

I continued meeting with our investors, and one by one, they joined us, with a promise to Jaye Dyer that we would not be back for ten years. The first major foundations to join us were Bush, McKnight, 3M, St. Paul Companies, Cargill, General Mills, and The St. Paul Foundation. After their commitments, many other investors joined us in creating a capital pool that would allow us to retool the entire corporation and be worthy of a $1,500,000 line of credit on our own. We were all so proud of one another!

It was very important to me that MDI embody the best kind of charity. Charity can be the most beautiful act we are capable of as members of society, or it can be as demeaning and dependence-creating as our welfare system has become. Charity is the responsibility of each of us, and it is only because we have abdicated our responsibility to be charitable to government that we have systems that so poorly serve the needy of our communities. I learned what true charity is from watching my parents demonstrate real charity when caring for one of our neighbors on Rice Street. The family next door was devastated financially and emotionally when the father left to live with someone else. It was in the winter and they had run out of coal, and in Minnesota you do not survive the winter without heat. My parents wanted to help, but only in a way where she and the children could maintain their dignity. They knew she was a very good baker, and they asked her if she would bake bread for them if they would order coal for her. My parents went on to explain that my mother did not have time to bake, now that Barbara, the last of the older five, had arrived. They also shared that no one in the family liked the bread you could buy at the store. She accepted, and every other day she would bring over that warm bread just out of the oven, with its never-to-be-forgotten aroma. Then we would experience the love she had for all of us. God has placed unlimited opportunities for each of us to express the core virtue of charity, and each of us has the opportunity to experience the love that those who are needy have to share with us.

Growing up is a lifelong process, and hopefully will be a part of whatever life is left for me. To understand growth, you must be able to recognize not only gross change in your life but also subtle refinements. Growth is not always linear. It's more than how much things change. It is also what kind of change. There were periods in my life when I grew professionally very rapidly, and regressed personally at the same time. We sometimes refer to that time as when we are "full of ourselves." When we have been successful and we become surrounded by cheerleaders, it is very easy to overlook some really inexcusable behaviors. We pull our professional achievements with us into our personal lives, where they have little or no value.

What accomplishments am I the most proud of? The first was when Howard Nelson asked me to design and teach a graduate course with him at the University of Minnesota's College of Education. Next was to teach a graduate course at the University of Arizona, Tucson, and then join the staff at York University in Canada to further develop this new discipline. Next came an invitation to lecture at University College at Oxford University in England. After writing and co-authoring five books, the discipline was finally defined by me as "social change through economic development." Speaking on this subject would take me all over the world, to such places as the Soviet Union and Japan. At the same time, we were building MDI into a showplace, to show what could be done when you shifted from delivering social services to creating economic opportunities for persons with a career disability. At the end, we had demonstrated that we could employ over 1,300 individuals and generate $58 million in commercial revenues annually with more that 62 percent of the employees having a severe disability. That is what I did. But just as important was the love I felt for so many individuals whom God kept putting in my way.

How sad it was to learn from John's son Jacques that John had passed away on March 6, 2008, from a ruptured blood vessel in his brain and subsequent stroke. We had been e-mailing back and forth just a few days earlier. As I wrestled with my thoughts I opened his book about the creation of MDI called *The Affirmative Enterprise*. In the introduction John writes, "Each of our contributions will be different, demonstrated by our unique talents and capabilities. Some will contribute by being business persons or teachers; others will contribute by learning to become responsible for something as basic as their own grooming and self-care. It is through the acceptance of our responsibilities, as dimensioned by our innate capacities, that each of us increases our value to ourselves and subsequently contributes to the communities in which we live." A memorial service was held in May at St. Francis de Sales Church in St. Paul, hosted by John's sisters and brothers. The program celebrated "John DuRand beloved husband, devoted father and brother to all. Accomplished entrepreneur, author, historian, carpenter, photographer, visionary, social innovator, professor, Prior, ski and golf instructor, founder and CEO of Minnesota Diversified Industries (MDI)."

EPILOGUE

One of the themes that emerges from these stories for me is that social entrepreneurs have all of the challenges of for-profit entrepreneurs, and then some. Yet they don't often get the recognition they so well deserve. Accounting systems have not yet been invented that easily display the value added by their work. Economic cycles can either bolster or seriously impair their fundraising capability. Boards of directors without adequate training in non-profit governance can at times restrain progress. The skills required at both the board and staff levels are significant, not to mention the compassion and discipline required to serve disadvantaged members of the community as clients.

What is most challenging for these leaders is that social problems are becoming ever more complex, even as government funds for addressing those problems are shrinking. As a result, social entrepreneurs face a continual need to bolster their marketing and general business management skills, so they can do more with less.

When I was in the investment business, there was no end to the inquiries about new public common stock offerings, especially those of favored growth stocks. Especially attractive was the financing of start-up companies that fit the popular trend or theme of the times. I never heard a complaint about the volume of public stock offerings. Much later, when I devoted my time to not-for-profit organizations, I would occasionally hear someone say, "These requests for money are driving me crazy…There are just too damned many non-profits."

Why is it that we sometimes resent the intrusions on our time and attention for entities we refer to as charities, when we often welcome the new information included in the prospectus of a publicly traded company? Perhaps it is because very little is taught in our journey through formal education about the essential role non-profits play in our community. It is often not made clear how society as a whole benefits from the work of the non-profit community. Evaluation techniques are still evolving, and the most popular and widely-used do not accurately define the economic contribution that a non-profit organization makes. To a great extent, we view non-profit organizations as groups that help someone else, but do not benefit ourselves in real economic terms.

I believe that view is mistaken. Economists now estimate that tax-exempt non-profits make up about 10 percent of the economy. What has not been quantified, but what is plainly evident, is how these organizations actually save the taxpayer money, create a high quality of life for us all, and build a climate in a community that allows businesses to prosper. Those of us with business backgrounds tend to take for granted the existence of well-trained workers, crime-free neighborhoods, affordable housing for employees, an expanding middle class of consumers, short commuting times to work, and pre-kindergarten through twelfth grade education systems that prepare our children to become contributing citizens.

One of the overwhelming demographic trends that will have a dramatic effect on our economy is the projected shortfall in skilled and semi-skilled workers over the next few decades. Another factor of concern to economists is the growing income gap between the wealthy in the United States and those in the lowest quartile of family income. Moving families out of poverty generates both new workers and new taxpayers, and the pursuit of that goal is, ultimately, the life work of each social entrepreneur profiled in this book. The common denominator is that they each help empower people, so that those people can fulfill their destiny, become self-sufficient, and contribute to the social and economic strength of our community.

I am struck by other things these individuals have in common. In each case, they were influenced by at least one positive role model, who set an example and nurtured that individual's development. They each exhibit a deep curiosity about how things work and about what motivates people to want to invest in community building. There is a unique skill involved in convincing a financial supporter that it is in their family's long-term interest to help empower those that have been less fortunate. What I also see in these stories is joy, a sense of humor about life's surprises, and awareness of their own limitations.

I find it especially interesting that none of these leaders set out on the path to adulthood with a goal of community service in mind. When the call came, they were well prepared, many with past experience in business and the professions. So what is it that creates these incredible social entrepreneurs? We can only speculate. For me, it has to be a curiosity instilled early in life about people and how they relate to one another. In addition, there is family, a sense of where one's roots are, that compels the passing along to others the gifts each inherited. Education and lifelong learning are also essential ingredients in the success of each of these individuals.

In many cases, someone intervened at just the right time to play the role of matchmaker. I refer to these people as the bridge builders. These are civic leaders from all walks of life who have the breadth of knowledge about their community to spot talent and recognize where it can be utilized. This aspect of their life's work is often done quietly, without public recognition. Their satisfaction comes from helping others succeed. In my opinion, that's the mark of a true professional.

One final theme that emerges from these inspiring stories is the financial support offered to them at varying times by members of the business and foundation community. The list of benefactors is long indeed; many are included in the index that follows. Despite competitive pressures, business leaders, including many CEO's, took time out of their day to listen to the community needs, as expressed by these non-profit leaders. They understood that they were being invited to invest in their own long-term self interest. They also took satisfaction from spotting a great community opportunity and making a bet, much like investing in the stock market. They would refer good projects to one another, and challenge each other at times to equal or exceed each others' gifts.

What a gift we have in these leaders from so many different backgrounds. Each in their own way represent the incredible opportunity the United States has to offer when the proper systems are in place to nurture professional development. As we have read, these systems come in many forms, including family, teachers, and mentors who are on the lookout for outstanding leaders.

My hope is that some who read these stories may come to play a part themselves in this region's world of non-profits, or help to identify and nurture the next generation of social entrepreneurs. Certainly the times demand it.

In the Twin Cities, we have recently had dramatic evidence of what happens when one kind of infrastructure fails, and a major bridge collapses. There is reason to believe that our social infrastructure also lacks proper maintenance, and is growing weaker. We see worrisome levels of failure in our educational systems, a lack of affordable housing, growing disparities in family incomes, violence in our urban centers, a growing shortage of skilled and semi-skilled workers, and the continued presence of racism. We must shore up our social infrastructure if we are to overcome these difficulties, and compete in a world in which the rate of change is accelerating. I am confident that we have the resources to do the job. But do we have the commitment and will to support the next generation of social entrepreneurs who can make it happen?

Social entrepreneurs lead us to do things we never dreamed possible. They can help us visualize a future filled with opportunity and progress, and convince us to overcome our political differences and to invest in that promising future accordingly. Let us each help it be so.

Appendix:

A List of Civic Leaders that Appear in the book

Beach, Tom. Former associate director of the Minneapolis Foundation.

Berger, Ben. Minneapolis business executive active in professional sports, with a wide range of philanthropic interests.

Bolger, John. President of Bolger Press and advocate for Minnesota's racial and ethnic minorities.

Brin, Fanny. The first United Nations Association chairperson in Minnesota and past President of the National Council of Jewish Women.

Cann, Jack. Twin Cities attorney whose clients include low-income housing organizations.

Carroll, John. Twin Cities business executive and philanthropist.

Christenson, Mike. Past head of the Allina Foundation; City of Minneapolis Director of CPED (community planning and economic development).

Conte, Dick. Past director of the Dayton Hudson Foundation.

Craig, Earl. African American leader; former executive director of the Urban Coalition, a non-profit organization advocating for human rights and social justice.

Cramer, Steve. Former staff member of the Urban Coalition; former member of the Minneapolis City Council; CEO of Project for Pride in Living.

Dayton, Mark. Early promoter of effective rural and urban economic development, philanthropist; U.S. senator, 2001-06.

Doermann, Humphrey. Founding president of the Bush Foundation; advocate for academic excellence in public education.

Dorsey, Peter. Twin Cities attorney, philanthropist and early sponsor and financial supporter of the Legal Rights Center.

Edwards, Ron. Civil rights activist from the near north side of Minneapolis.

Egan, Harvey. Pastor of St. Joan of Arc Catholic Church in south Minneapolis; and leading clergy voice for social justice, peacemaking and human rights.

Ewald, Russ. Served as president of both the Minneapolis and McKnight Foundations; credited for solutions to problems impacting rural and urban areas..

Fashiana, Gene. St. Paul businessman and community activist.

Finzell, Greg. Executive director of the Rondo Community Land Trust; former director of the Summit-University Planning Council in St. Paul and the Hawthorne Area Community Council in Minneapolis.

Flahavan, Ed. Former pastor of St. Stephen's Catholic Church in south Minneapolis and a leader in the social justice activities of the Archdiocese of St. Paul and Minneapolis.

Flory, John. Leader of the Whittier Neighborhood Community Development Corporation.

Fraser, Don. U.S. Congressman, 1962-78; Mayor of Minneapolis, 1980-1993; advocate for early childhood education and neighborhood revitalization.

Gabler, Joe. Former director of the Minneapolis office of the U.S. Department of Housing and Urban Development; pioneer of innovative approaches to developing affordable housing.

Glover, Gleason. Civil rights activist; former head of the Minneapolis Urban League.

Hale, Roger. Retired CEO of the Tennant Company; activist on behalf of communities of color and the disenfranchised.

Harmon, Ruell. St Paul business executive and political activist: an early advocate for improving Minnesota's criminal justice system.

Hartzell, Tom. St Paul corporate CEO and philanthropist; supporter of efforts to train prospective workers with mental and physical disabilities.

Haskin, David. Minneapolis business executive who provided advice and leadership to the Citizens Council on Crime and Justice.

Helfeld, Ed. Former head of St. Paul's Housing and Redevelopment Authority.

Heltzer, Jim. Former director of the Minneapolis Community Development Agency and former state Economic Development director; Beltrami County commissioner.

Hetland, James. Executive with U.S. Bank who became the first head of the Greater Twin Cities Metropolitan Council.

Hubbs, Ron. Past CEO of the St. Paul Companies; Twin Cities philanthropist.

Humphrey, Bill. Former General Mills executive with broad philanthropic interests, particularly in combating racism and promoting economic justice.

Jeans, Dan. Business owner, civic fundraiser, leader of the North End Neighborhood Business Association.

Krusell, Chuck. Served as Executive Director of the Minneapolis Housing and Redevelopment Authority; president of the Minneapolis Chamber of Commerce; advocate for innovative affordable housing programs.

Latimer, George. Mayor of St. Paul, 1976-1990; Dean, Hamline Law School; Distinguished Visiting Professor of Urban Affairs, Macalester College; affordable housing authority.

Latimer, Nancy. Senior program officer, McKnight Foundation; pioneer of innovative ways to move families out of poverty, and early advocate for quality early childhood education.

Le Fluer, Fred. Former Minnesota Commissioner of Corrections; Hennepin County Corrections Administrator.

Lilly, R.C. St. Paul business executive and philanthropist who took a special interest in non-profit organizations promoting self-sufficiency.

Linares, Juan. Community organizer and neighborhood development consultant in St. Paul.

McCannel, Louise. Heir to the P. B. Walker timber fortune and one of the first in the Twin Cities to assist young African Americans to organize and advocate for change.

McKinley, Ron. One of the first Native Americans to gain prominence in professional philanthropy as a senior program officer with leading Twin Cities community and private foundations.

McLaughlin, Peter. Former staff member of the Urban Coalition; Minnesota House; 1985-1990 Hennepin County Commissioner, 1991-present.

Messenger, Bill. Minneapolis attorney; social justice and human rights advocate.

Mgeni, Yusef. Minneapolis Urban Coalition director, 1989-2001; Director of Educational Equity, St. Paul Public Schools; advocate for racial equality and economic justice.

Miranda, Sal. Administrator of Interfaith Action, a social justice organization.

Mullaney, Frank. Cofounder, Cray Research Corp. and Control Data Corp.

Murphy, Ruth. Founder of the Community Design Center, which creates models for success in blighted neighborhoods in the Twin Cities.

Nasby, David. Former Director of the City Inc, a teenage drop-in center and alternative school; retired Associate Director of the General Mills Foundation.

Nyberg, Luanne. Former head of the Children's Defense Fund-Minnesota; has held a variety of public and private policy leadership posts, including staff of the Minnesota attorney general.

O'Keefe, Michael. President of the McKnight Foundation, 1988-1998; state commissioner of human services, 1998-2002; president of the Minneapolis College of Art and Design.

Pacheco, John. Director, Xcel Energy Foundation.

Palmer, Bruce. Retired head of community affairs for Northern States Power Company (today, Xcel Energy).

Plank, Ray. Founder and CEO of Apache Corporation, a leader in oil exploration, with philanthropic interests in education and civil rights.

Prchal, Dennis. St. Paul insurance businessman, active in North End Area Rivitalization Inc., and other civic improvement efforts.

Rapson, Rip. Former deputy mayor of Minneapolis; past president of the McKnight Foundation; president of the Kresge Foundation.

Rekstad, Howard. Founder and president of a St. Paul-based real estate development and management company.

Renier, James. Retired CEO of Honeywell; pioneer in Twin Cities early childhood education and founder of "Success By Six."

Sands, Bill. Retired chairman of Western Bank; developed creative approaches to promoting, managing and financing urban renewal.

Scribner, Duane. Former senior program officer, Dayton Hudson Foundation.

Selvaggio, Joe. Former priest who founded Project for Pride in Living and other organizations serving the disadvantaged. He formed the One Percent Club which encourages individuals to give from their net worth.

Shannon, Jim. Former priest and auxiliary bishop, Archdiocese of St. Paul and Minneapolis; President of the University (then College) of St Thomas; left the active priesthood over the issue of birth control; headed both the Minneapolis and General Mills Foundations.

Verette, Paul. Entrepreneurial and creative former head of the St. Paul Foundation.

Warder, John. The first African American to head a bank in Minnesota; first African American on the Minneapolis School Board; instrumental in the revitalization of north Minneapolis following riots in 1966 and 1967.

Zulu, Vusi. African American leader; KMOJ radio personality; force for positive change in north Minneapolis.

INDEX

W

Y

Z

ABOUT THE AUTHOR

A Minneapolis native, Peter Heegaard began his business career in Minneapolis in 1960 with the Trust Group of Northwestern National Bank of Minneapolis, which he headed from 1980 to 1986. He was the founder and former Managing Principal of Lowry Hill, a subsidiary of Wells Fargo. He retired in 1996 to serve as a consultant and community volunteer to several foundations and non-profit organizations.

In 1997 he founded Urban Adventure, a Twin Cities-based educational program that exposes young leaders in business and MBA candidates to our most challenging urban issues. A key objective of the program is to use community agencies to illustrate the economic advantages of rebuilding neighborhoods and training people for living-wage jobs. He also edits *An Investment Letter for Minnesota Philanthropists*, a quarterly publication that focuses on the benefits non-profit organizations can provide to their local communities and the state of Minnesota.

Heegaard is active in a wide range of civic organizations. He currently serves as chair of Ready 4 K and is on the boards of the Northstar Foundation and the One Percent Club. He has served on the boards of a wide range of organizations including the Charles K. Blandin Foundation, the Gamble Skogmo Foundation, Wolf Ridge Environmental Learning Center, the Minneapolis Foundation, Presbyterian Homes of Minnesota, the Hennepin County Library Board, and the Legal Rights Center.

Heegaard is a member of Plymouth Congregational Church and a former member of St. Luke Presbyterian Church, where he served as elder. His favorite pastimes include fly fishing, hiking, skiing and biking. Heegaard lives with his wife, Anne, in Minneapolis, Minnesota. They have three children and eight grandchildren.